SCREENING THE SYSTEM

Screening the System

*Exposing Security
Clearance Dangers*

MARTHA LOUISE DEUTSCHER

POTOMAC BOOKS
An imprint of the University of Nebraska Press

∞

Library of Congress Cataloging-in-
Publication Data
Names: Deutscher, Martha Louise.
Title: Screening the system: exposing
security clearance dangers / Martha
Louise Deutscher.
Description: Lincoln: Potomac Books,
an imprint of the University of Nebraska
Press, 2017. | Includes bibliographical
references and index.
Identifiers: LCCN 2016020359 (print) |
LCCN 2016033879 (ebook) |
ISBN 9781612348131 (hardback: alk.
paper) | ISBN 9781612348766 (epub) |
ISBN 9781612348773 (mobi) |
ISBN 9781612348780 (pdf)
Subjects: LCSH: Security clearances—
United States. | National security—
United States. | BISAC: POLITICAL
SCIENCE / Political Freedom &
Security / Intelligence.
Classification: LCC JK734 .D48 2017
(print) | LCC JK734 (ebook) |
DDC 352.3/79—dc23
LC record available at https://lccn.loc.gov
/2016020359

Set in Minion by Westchester Publishing
Services.

CONTENTS

ILLUSTRATIONS

ACKNOWLEDGMENTS

I wish to thank my doctoral committee in the Cultural Studies Department at George Mason University. Dr. Hugh Gusterson provided valuable guidance as my advisor and as the first reader of my doctoral thesis on this subject. I also wish to thank Professors Roger Lancaster and Peter Mandaville for their support during my research.

This book is dedicated to my mother Verda Deutscher who instilled in me her love of reading and of books. I am most grateful to my father, Irwin Deutscher, for reading the first draft of the manuscript and providing helpful feedback.

Finally, this book would not have been possible without the federal workers who shared their stories with me. Many had to revisit painful histories, and I am enormously grateful to them for taking the risk. Regrettably, I cannot acknowledge them by name, but their courage, resilience, and patriotism remain an inspiration to me.

INTRODUCTION

This book critically examines the personnel security clearance system, the process by which the federal government incorporates individuals into secret national security work, and how individuals experience the process. I pay particular attention to the ways in which security clearance practices discipline and transform individuals who are subject to them. Using the voices of the system's participants, I explore the relationship between individual workers and state power as articulated in the personnel security clearance process.

I believe the public debate on security policy in general—and on the personnel security clearance system in particular—requires a new and more imaginative discussion if it is to improve. Discussions to date have been dominated by bureaucrats, security professionals, and politicians, who tend to treat the problems in the system with the same archaic policies and practices they have used in the past—with the same flawed results.

To the best of my knowledge, this is the only study to date that examines the impact of the national personnel security clearance system on the hearts and minds of both those who are subject to it and those who are tasked to maintain it. Although the book is based on my doctoral dissertation at George Mason University, I undertook this study for personal reasons. All science is part biography. I began my civil service career in 1990 with the United States Information Agency and held positions of increasing responsibility in the Departments of State and Defense continuously until I retired from federal service in 2013.

During that time, I held and maintained security clearances at various levels and was subject to the system I describe. I have been investigated and interviewed (although never polygraphed), and I participated in the investigation of others during federal service. I never lost a clearance or had one revoked.

My federal career focused on many aspects of security policy. While at the State Department, I conducted international public diplomacy programs for the Voice of America and for the U.S. Agency for International Development.

At the Defense Department, one of my positions was legislative and public affairs director for the Department of Defense Security Service, the entity responsible for administering the National Industrial Security Program. That program administers the security clearance processes for the U.S. defense industry and the contractors employed within it. As the chief communications officer for the agency, my contact information was online, and I was easy to find. Many people called me with complaints about having lost a security clearance and consequently their jobs. I listened to their stories. I heard anger, fear, anxiety, and a full mix of human sentiment. Such emotion suggested to me at the time that the hurt resulting from losing one's security clearance was more than financial. The more I listened, the more I learned that one loses more than a career when one loses a clearance. I began to realize that I wanted to learn more about what had befallen these workers. So I undertook to study the clearance system by talking with those who had run afoul of it.

I begin with a brief history of perceived national security threats in the United States and the policies that were put in place to address them. These threats have at times included specific subsets of Americans, including government employees. I also review some of the many types of human threats that the clearance system is designed to reduce.

I then turn to the processes by which individuals are inducted into national security jobs. To describe the system, I use documentary sources from federal government websites, including those of the United States Departments of Defense, State, Treasury, Agriculture, and Homeland Security. I also reference legislation, executive orders, policy guidance and government security handbooks, and other such materials. Next I review the mechanisms used to process individuals through the clearance system. I also draw on some examples, from contemporary news reporting, of how the system sometimes fails those within it. I employ news reports as secondary sources; approached with judicious caution, they provide context to some of the debate surrounding the personnel security clearance process. And I have tried to choose the most reliable reporting.

We currently lack a scientifically rigorous and consistent way of judging people. Much of the clearance process has proven to be flawed. For this reason, trustworthy employees are sometimes wrongly removed from federal positions while spies and other potential threats remain in their jobs undetected.

I interviewed people over a two-year period about their experiences with the national personnel security clearance system. I interviewed individuals who ran afoul of the system, some of whom lost their clearances. I also interviewed those who support them—lawyers, family members, and counselors. In addition, I interviewed security practitioners and specialists and other individuals who currently hold a clearance, and I used the transcripts of these interviews to bolster my observations.

I also tried to glean from the interviews what people's individual experiences can teach us about the power relationship between the individual and the state. The interviews are intimate glances into personal experiences, but they demonstrate larger societal structures at work in the areas of national security and state power. The study investigates, through documentary sources and interviews, how the security clearance process was shaped and also how it shapes identity. All interviews were conducted in confidence. To maintain my interview subjects' anonymity, I have used pseudonyms in quoting their responses and describing their experiences.

I make no claims to have selected a representative sample. While I am aware of the methodological limitations of my process, I believe, based in part on my own experience working for the federal government, that what these people have articulated illuminates the complex power relationship between individuals and the state that they swore to serve. Most federal workers never lose a security clearance, so these individual experiences are not the standard.

Descriptions of being "blacklisted" by one's community are a poignant reference to one of our country's darker moments, the anti-Communist hysteria of the 1950s now known as the Red Scare.[1] Mention by some respondents of "wearing a scarlet letter" after losing a clearance is another singularly American reference, both literary and historic. The Puritanism of Nathaniel Hawthorne's novel *The Scarlet Letter,* and which Max Weber observed underlying the spirit of capitalism, also infuses individuals within the personnel security clearance system (which falls squarely within that capitalist system) with the sense of dread that accompanies misplaced or erroneous societal judgment and corresponding punitive measures.[2]

Workers who personally experience the imbalance of power between the individual and the state do not soon forget it. Fiction writers, including Hawthorne, Franz Kafka, Arthur Miller, and Joseph Heller, provide artistic insights into this very real social drama.[3] My informants agree that the system should undergo improvements, but almost all believe that such a system is necessary. Their concurrence speaks eloquently to the underlying American belief in national security and the state's need to keep secrets, as articulated in the national personnel security clearance system. This belief is held firmly even by those to whom the system has been unkind.

I conclude by offering some recommendations based on what I learned from my research. By critiquing the personnel security clearance system, my aim is not to imply that a national security apparatus is not important. Nation-states have a legitimate need for secrets and secrecy. But I have come to believe that the personnel security clearance apparatus, like other bureaucracies of power, has a tendency to outgrow its legitimate need. Part of the reason secrecy is problematic is that secrets are so hard to keep. So in addition to the flaws in the current system, the sheer number of clearance holders is, in and of itself, a threat. Without denying the need for some kind of secrecy bureaucracy, I explore the defects of that bureaucracy, which include a proclivity for capriciousness, imprudence, prejudice, unfairness, and intimidation. By interviewing people who have dedicated their careers to the service of their country, I learned how they react when the national security apparatus of a country founded on constitutional rights and due process eschews those values in the treatment of its own employees. The research suggests that such practices within the security clearance system may contribute to the insecurity that the system is designed to mitigate. What happens when a process constructed around tropes of rationality turns irrational? What happens when the national security apparatus of a country dedicated to constitutional rights and due process denies the due process rights of its own employees? How do people who have given their careers to the service of their country's ideals react when, in the name of those ideals, they see their careers destroyed by the rejection of those same ideals? How do systems of security promote insecurity? These are the questions explored in the succeeding chapters.

I hope that this study contributes to a more robust understanding of the role of individuals in the security clearance process and enhances future discussions of improvements to the process.

ABBREVIATIONS

ACES	Automated Continuing Evaluation System
ADS	Adjudication Decision Support System
BI	background investigation
BTA	Business Transformation Agency (Department of Defense)
CAF	Central Adjudication Facility
CIA	Central Intelligence Agency
DoD	U.S. Department of Defense
DCII	Defense Central Index of Investigations System
DHRA	Defense Human Resources Activity
DIA	Defense Intelligence Agency
DIMHRS	Defense Integrated Military Human Resources System
DISA	Defense Information Systems Agency
DMDC	Defense Manpower Data Center
DNI	director of national intelligence
DOE	U.S. Department of Energy
DOHA	Defense Office of Hearings and Appeals
DOJ	U.S. Department of Justice
DSS	Diplomatic Security Service (Department of State)
EPPA	Employee Polygraph Protection Act of 1988
FBI	Federal Bureau of Investigation
HUAC	House Un-American Activities Committee
GAO	U.S. General Accounting Office

JPAS	Joint Personnel Adjudication System (Department of Defense)
JROTC	Junior Reserve Officers Training Corps
IC	intelligence community
ICAF	Industrial College of the Armed Forces
IEHR	Integrated Electronic Health Record (Department of Defense and Department of Veterans Affairs)
IRR	Investigative Records Repository, also referred to as the "Improved" Investigative Records Repository (iIRR)
IRTPA	Intelligence Reform and Terrorism Prevention Act
IT	information technology
NAVSEA	Naval Sea Systems Command
NCCA	National Center for Credibility Assessment (Department of Defense)
NGA	National Geospatial-Intelligence Agency
NOC	non-official cover
NRO	National Reconnaissance Office
NSA	National Security Agency
OIG	Office of the Inspector General
OPM	Office of Personnel Management
OTA	Office of Technology Assessment (U.S. Congress)
PARM	Post-Adjudication Risk Management Plan (FBI)
PDD	Psychophysiological Detection of Deception Program
PERSEREC	Personnel and Security Research Center (Department of Defense)
PR	periodic reinvestigation
SCIF	Sensitive Compartmented Information Facility
SES	Senior Executive Service
SF-86	standard form and questionnaire for national security positions
SSBI	single-scope background investigation
SWFT	Secure Web Fingerprint Transmission Program
USIS	United States Investigations Services

SCREENING THE SYSTEM

1   The Many Faces of a Threat

When granting a security clearance, the state seeks to screen out those who cannot be trusted with secrets. In order to do so, the security clearance system demands that all participants in the system take for granted foundational assumptions that naturalize the national security needs of the state, the security clearance system, and its processes.

At times throughout U.S. history, specific groups of people, including federal workers, have been perceived as threats to national security. War, international alliances, sabotage, surprise attacks, and leaks have all shaped national security priorities as well as the lives of those entrusted to serve the state. In this section, I briefly explain how some perceived threats to the national security have evolved.

What quickly becomes evident is the multifaceted nature of the threat to national security and the magnitude of the workload for those required to keep secrets safe. Every time a federal employee commits a violent act in the workplace people ask, "How did he get a security clearance?" Every time an employee leaks secrets to the press or commits espionage, the same question arises. The state must defend against a plethora of current and potential obstacles using its current security clearance apparatus. Just as military planners are chastised for fighting the last war, it is the tendency of personnel security bureaucrats to rely on existing and familiar tactics. But it is important for those responsible for the clearance system to look for better technologies and methodologies with which to keep secrets safe. Just like snowflakes, no two individuals are exactly alike, and predicting human behavior is tricky.

The Cold War and the Red and Lavender Scares

From George Washington's time on, presidential administrations have grappled with ways to promote national security while mitigating security threats. When John Adams became president in 1797, his national security concerns were shaped by a war between the French and the British that caused intense partisanship among contending factions within the United States. Adams feared political unrest abroad might influence secession movements at home. He voiced his national security concerns to Congress, which authorized raising a provisional army. Congress also passed the Alien and Sedition Acts, intended to frighten foreign agents into leaving the country and stifle attacks on the administration by the opposition press. Among other things, the acts forbade any individual or group to oppose "any measure or measures of the United States." Under the Sedition Act, it was illegal to say, write, or print anything about the president that brought him "into contempt or disrepute." Four major newspapers were charged with sedition just before the presidential election of 1800, and several foreign-born journalists were threatened with expulsion. The attorney general charged seventeen people with sedition, and ten were convicted.

Benjamin Franklin Bache, a grandson of Benjamin Franklin and editor of the *Philadelphia Aurora* newspaper, was charged with "libeling the President and the Executive Government in a manner tending to excite sedition and opposition to the laws." Bache had written an editorial referring to the president as "old, querulous, bald, blind, crippled, toothless Adams."[1] While one can understand why Bache was persona non grata at the Adams White House, it is easy to see why his arrest led to a public outcry against the Alien and Sedition Acts and contributed to the election, in 1800, of Thomas Jefferson. Jefferson pardoned all those convicted under the Sedition Act, and Congress returned all fines paid, with interest.

Not until the twentieth century did espionage emerge again as a national security priority. President Woodrow Wilson signed the

Espionage Act of 1917 two months after the United States entered World War I in response to German agents blowing up a munitions dump in New York Harbor. As during previous wars, hysteria surrounding foreign agents ensued. In addition to the Espionage Act, in 1918 Congress passed another Sedition Act, criminalizing, among other things, "abusive language" about the government.

Although some of the most important legislation associated with national security predates World War I, it is the Cold War that familiarized most Americans with the concept of a security clearance.

The Cold War

As the new Soviet enemy emerged after World War II, national security priorities focused on preventing government employees from sharing secrets with that enemy. The emphasis in the Eisenhower administration was on keeping its nuclear secrets. But J. Robert Oppenheimer, the nation's most famous nuclear scientist, called on the government to release nuclear secrets. Oppenheimer had headed the Manhattan Project, a secret weapons program that developed, tested, and made possible the use of the first atomic weapons during World War II. But in February 1953 he gave a speech arguing that, rather than keeping any discussion of the nuclear program secret, it was actually more candor that was required in the service of national security.[2] Indeed Oppenheimer believed that the only way to avoid an arms race was to share scientific knowledge with the Soviet Union. According to Kai Bird and Martin Sherwin, Oppenheimer's ideas were in the minority and not at all well accepted in Washington: "It is hard to imagine a more provocative speech. . . . Here was a celebrated private citizen, armed with the highest security clearance, denigrating the secrecy that surrounded the nation's war plans. As word spread through Washington's national security bureaucracy of what Oppenheimer had said, many were appalled."[3]

So in retrospect it is no surprise that on December 21, 1953, Oppenheimer was told that his security clearance had been suspended, pending resolution of a series of charges, and he was asked to resign. Oppenheimer chose not to resign and requested a hearing instead. The hearing that followed in April and May of 1954 focused on Oppenheimer's past Communist ties and his association, during the Manhattan Project, with suspected disloyal or Communist scientists. When the outcomes of the hearings were later made public, Americans learned that the Atomic Energy Commission had revoked the security clearance of the "father of the atomic bomb."

Part of the reason that Oppenheimer's hearings were of such interest to the public was that 1953 was also the year Julius and Ethel Rosenberg were executed after having been convicted of espionage for passing atomic secrets to the Soviets.[4] The Rosenberg case garnered worldwide attention. The Rosenbergs' supporters claimed they were being made scapegoats to the "Red Scare" then sweeping America. The French writer and philosopher Jean-Paul Sartre called their execution a "legal lynching."[5] Sartre and others pointed out that even if the Rosenbergs did pass secrets to the Soviets during World War II, Russia had been an ally, not an enemy, of the United States at the time. Irrespective of their relative guilt, the Rosenbergs' execution galvanized the attention of the American public to the retaliation of the state against its employees charged with espionage and treason.

The Red Scare

As noted, both the Oppenheimer and the Rosenberg hearings were entangled with the ongoing national Red Scare and the Cold War. But near the end of World War II, the national security priority was to win the war, in part by beating the Axis powers to the development of an atomic bomb and then by using it against them. So the threat that government workers posed was perceived to be classic espionage—the direct disclosure of nuclear secrets to the nation's enemies (Germany and Japan).

But with the advance of the Cold War, the national security threat had crystallized against the Soviet Union—a former ally. When Russia built its own bomb (partly with secrets supplied through espionage), the perceived threat was that federal workers might be "fellow travelers" or Communists with sympathies toward the Soviet Union and its quest for a global commune.

Beginning in 1950, Senator Joseph Raymond "Joe" McCarthy became the public face of Cold War tensions by fueling fears of Communist conspiracies and subversion among federal workers and others. He claimed that there were large numbers of Communists and Soviet spies and sympathizers inside federal government entities and industries. McCarthy rose to national fame in February 1950 when he asserted in a speech that he had a list of members of the Communist Party and members of a spy ring employed in the U.S. State Department.

Although he was never able to prove those charges, he continued to claim that Communists had infiltrated the Truman administration's State Department, the Voice of America, and the United States Army. He also used various charges of Communism, Communist sympathies, disloyalty, and homosexuality to attack politicians and other individuals inside and outside of government. One of the most publicized and notable examples of McCarthy's tactics during his House Un-American Activities Committee (HUAC) hearings was the compilation of "blacklists," particularly in the entertainment industry where celebrity informants (like then–Screen Actors Guild President Ronald Reagan) were encouraged to report to the committee on the political activities of fellow actors, writers, directors, and others in the industry. Many of those accused lost their jobs in the process.[6]

The Lavender Scare

Not as widely known as McCarthy's anti-Communist crusade were his various attempts to intimidate, and expel from government positions, persons whom he accused, or threatened to publicly accuse, of homosexuality. Former U.S. senator Alan K. Simpson has written: "The so-called 'Red Scare' has been the main focus of most historians of that period of time. A lesser-known element . . . and one that harmed far more people was the witch-hunt McCarthy and others conducted against homosexuals."[7]

The genesis of Simpson's observation may have been Eisenhower's Executive Order 10450, which revoked Truman's 1947 Executive

Order 9835, sometimes called the Loyalty Order. Truman's order had stated, "There shall be a loyalty investigation of every person entering the civilian employment of any department or agency of the executive branch of the Federal Government." But Eisenhower's new Executive Order 10450 charged the heads of federal agencies and the Office of Personnel Management, supported by the Federal Bureau of Investigation (FBI), with investigating federal employees to determine not only if they were loyal to the United States but also whether they posed "security risks." And it expanded the definitions and conditions used to make such determinations.

Previously, the criteria used to define a security risk within the federal workforce were political, including affiliation with suspect organizations, aiding and abetting the enemy, sympathizing with subversives, and other clear demonstrations of disloyalty. And as noted earlier, during the Adams and Wilson administrations the perceived threat was from foreign influences such as saboteurs. Executive Order 10450 expanded the definition of what a security threat, in the form of a government worker, might look like. These included estimations of character and lifestyle choices: "Any criminal, infamous, dishonest, immoral, or notoriously disgraceful conduct, habitual use of intoxicants to excess, drug addiction, or sexual perversion."

Another notable impact of Executive Order 10450 was that Truman's earlier order had applied only to the State Department and selected military agencies. Eisenhower's new order extended to all employees of the federal government, including the military. David Johnson describes the impact of the new order and the resignation or firing of more than eight hundred federal employees in the two years between 1953 and 1955 whose files contained information about "sexual perversion."[8]

The purge, which took place in government and the defense industry, was comprehended by some (although not by many) at the time as the disaster that it was. Johnson writes that there were also those who understood the personal devastation that federal employees endured under the purge. "Almost no corporation or other private business will hire a man with such a stigma on his record," warned a prominent Washington psychiatrist. "If the present wave of public sentiment continues, certain male and female homosexuals will become persons without a country, since they may find it practically impossible to earn a living."[9]

The Crittenden Report

The misplaced enmity toward lesbian, gay, bisexual, and transgender (LGBT) federal workers was outlined by the Board Appointed to Prepare and Submit Recommendations to the Secretary of the Navy for the Revision of Policies, Procedures and Directives Dealing With homosexuals. In a report that was later dubbed the "Crittenden Report," named for the admiral who headed the board, it evaluated Navy policies dealing with homosexual personnel. Those policies were based in part on assertions made in a December 1950 Senate report of the Investigations Subcommittee of the Senate Committee on Expenditure in Executive Departments, which said that all of the government's intelligence agencies "are in complete agreement that sex perverts in Government constitute security risks."[10]

The Crittenden Report, by contrast, concluded that there was "no sound basis for the belief that homosexuals posed a security risk" and criticized the Senate report: "No intelligence agency, as far as can be learned, adduced any factual data before that committee with which to support these opinions," and said that "the concept that homosexuals necessarily pose a security risk is unsupported by adequate factual data." The Crittenden Report remained secret until 1976. Navy officials claimed they had no record of studies of homosexuality, but attorneys learned of its existence and obtained it through a Freedom of Information Act request.[11]

Clinton and Executive Order 12968

In 1995, President William Jefferson Clinton signed Executive Order 12968 establishing uniform policies for the assignment and administration of personnel security clearances and access to classified information. The order's antidiscrimination statement, "The United States Government does not discriminate on the basis of race, color, religion, sex, national origin, disability, or sexual orientation in granting access to classified information," was important because it included "sexual orientation" for the first time in an executive order. It also stipulates that "no inference" about suitability for access to classified information "may be raised solely on the basis of the sexual orientation of the employee."

The federal government had, at least since the Eisenhower administration and probably before, wrongly assumed that homosexuality was a disqualifying factor for holding a security clearance, despite the opposite findings of the U.S. Navy's Crittenden Report in 1957 and many others since.[12] But there had never been any data to back up the discrimination against homosexuals. Clinton's order not to discriminate on the basis of sexual orientation in granting access to classified information was important because it put to rest the blackmail rationale for declining clearance to LGBT Americans.

After Clinton's order, the Central Intelligence Agency (CIA) actively began recruiting LGBT Americans by cosponsoring networking events with them. According to the CIA, the agency is one of the founding partners of Outserve, an organization that provides legal aid and other resources to gay active-duty military personnel. In a recruiting event in Miami in 2012, Michael Barber, the CIA's LGBT community outreach and liaison program manager, said, "Part of the reason we're doing outreach is . . . that this is no longer an issue for holding security clearance, that we want the best and the brightest regardless of your sexual orientation."[13]

President Obama, in his 2012 State of the Union address, said, "When you put on that uniform, it doesn't matter if you're black or white; Asian, Latino, Native American; conservative, liberal; rich, poor; gay, straight. When you're marching into battle, you look out for the person next to you, or the mission fails." That year also marked the first ever Department of Defense Pride Month celebration, where Secretary of Defense Leon Panetta addressed a full auditorium at the Pentagon via video message saying, "As we recognize Pride month, I want to personally thank all of our gay and lesbian service members, LGBT civilians, and their families for their dedicated service to our country."[14]

As a result of this about-face, the pressure may be off LGBT individuals who seek to hold a security clearance. The same is not true for other segments of the federal workforce.

Ethnicity, Nationality, and Other Threats

When Japanese planes attacked Pearl Harbor on December 7, 1941, Franklin Roosevelt's national security priority shifted to organizing the nation for global war. Before Pearl Harbor, the FBI was already tracking elements and organizations that were suspected of loyalty to Germany, Japan, or Italy, and many people were arrested in the weeks after; seven thousand German and Italian aliens (non–U.S. citizens) were moved away from their homes on or near the West Coast and, along with 110,000 people of Japanese heritage (most of whom were U.S. citizens), put into "war relocation camps." Americans of Japanese descent were also banned from joining the military at the time. For example, Daniel Inouye, future Medal of Honor recipient and U.S. senator, was only allowed to serve as a medical volunteer in his home state of Hawaii when the war broke out. But in 1943, when the U.S. Army dropped its enlistment ban on Japanese Americans, Inouye enlisted in the 442nd Regimental Combat Team, a U.S. Army unit of second-generation Japanese Americans.[15] Many Americans of Japanese descent who had been previously interned with their families volunteered to serve their country.

Just as the ethnicity of specific citizens was seen as a threat during World War II, so are certain groups of federal workers undergoing undue scrutiny in the twenty-first century. The FBI's Post-Adjudication Risk Management Plan, or PARM roster, has more than doubled since its inception after terrorist attacks on the United States in 2001. The program singles out hundreds of FBI employees who were born overseas or have connections abroad for additional surveillance, ostensibly to prevent foreign spies from recruiting them. Authorities say that federal employees with foreign connections can pose potential national security risks. But they are speculating, as they have done throughout U.S. history when specific groups of people, including categories of federal workers, have been identified as threats to the state. I believe that one way to mitigate actual security risks is to reassess the assumptions underlying programs like PARM. Authorities have been wrong in the past about who poses a national security risk. For example, there are those thousands of federal workers who lost security clearances and jobs during the Cold War because they were gay. In the quest for security, a nation of immigrants must rely on the better angels of our nature that reject, rather than perpetuate, xenophobic predispositions.

In the case of the FBI's PARM program, the government may be working against its best interests. The United States needs diverse and talented employees. A report to the president and the Congress by the U.S. Merit Systems Protection Board in January 2013 states that employees of the federal government and applicants for employment should receive fair and equitable treatment in all aspects of personnel management "without regard to political affiliation, race, color, religion, national origin, sex, marital status, age, or handicapping condition, and with proper regard for their privacy and constitutional rights."[16] Senior FBI officials insist that inclusion in the PARM program is neither discriminatory nor a barrier to career advancement. Yet it is the rare individual who runs afoul of the security clearance system and emerges unscathed. And many at the FBI feel their careers have been hampered because of the very skills they were hired for possessing, such as languages and regional and cultural familiarity.

Looking for Traitors

The state must defend against a plethora of existing and potential obstacles using its security clearance apparatus. But there is no scientific method for predicting human behavior; and even if there were, it would be hard to address the diversity of threats with a single system of processes or procedures since there may be as many ways to betray one's country as there are individuals who serve it. Instead, the task of the personnel security clearance system is to try to predict which individuals will fall prey to their own human foibles. Although it is impossible to list the full spectrum of risk, below I have outlined some broad categories of human threat for consideration.

Spying for Love

Sharon Scranage was an American CIA secretary serving in Accra, Ghana, in the mid-1980s. The Ghanaian government used a young male Ghanaian intelligence officer to romance her in order to solicit intelligence. Scranage gave classified information to her lover, disclosing the identities of undercover CIA agents working in Ghana and plans for a coup against the Ghanaian government. Congress had previously passed the Intelligence Identities Protection Act in 1982, making it illegal to disclose "the identities of or personal information about intelligence officers." She was charged in July 1985 and in November was sentenced to five years' imprisonment, a term that was later reduced to two years.

Scranage is often held up as a warning about the dangers of romantic involvements with foreign nationals. But as Toby Harnden learned by interviewing former female CIA operatives for London's *Daily Telegraph*, those warnings seem to focus almost exclusively on women operatives. "Several of five CIA women interviewed said there was an institutional view that women were weaker than men and therefore more vulnerable to a 'honeypot' lure by foreign agents. Sheila, who was forced to resign when she announced she wanted to marry her European boyfriend, who had already been cleared by the CIA after she reported him as a friend, said: 'The honeypot threat was always being rammed down our throats. During the first three months of my training, the Sharon Scranage case must have been mentioned eight times.'"[17]

There is precedent for this type of thinking. The Stasi (Ministerium für Staatssicherheit), the former East German intelligence service, had a "Romeo network" consisting of agents assigned to develop long-term relationships with their sources during the Cold War. Women were the principal targets—often secretaries in Bonn's ministries and other government offices. The Stasi believed that one well-placed woman could prove more valuable than multiple male diplomats. According to Stasi officials, "They knew everything, and were often also responsible for their bosses' private correspondence."[18]

Spying for Money

Some individuals betray their country for love. For others, the reasons are more banal. Some people spy for money, like Robert Philip Hanssen. Hanssen is a former FBI agent who spied for Soviet and Russian intelligence services against the United States for twenty-two years, from 1979 to 2001. In 2002 he was sentenced to fifteen consecutive life sentences, and his betrayal has been described by the U.S. Department of Justice's Commission for the Review of FBI Security Programs as "possibly the worst intelligence disaster in U.S. history."[19] Hanssen sold secrets to the USSR and later Russia for more than $1.4 million in cash and diamonds. According to the Department of Defense, "Each of Hanssen's three periods of espionage was triggered by financial needs. When he contacted the Soviets in 1979, he was overwhelmed by the financial pressures of living in New York and providing for his growing family. He recontacted them in 1985 when he needed to pay off a $50,000 balloon mortgage on his home. In 1999, he was paying for private school education for his six children. His spending continually outstripped his income, even though his salary was near the top of the FBI pay scale."[20] When asked in an interview with CNN about his motivation to conduct espionage, Hanssen replied "Well, the reasons that I did what I did . . . were personal, banal, and amounted really to kind of greed and folly. As simple as that. The ability to decide to do that in order to make some quick and easy money, at very low risk."

Aldrich Ames, a thirty-one-year CIA counterintelligence officer and analyst, committed espionage by sharing secret documents and revealing to the Soviet Union the identities of at least twelve secret agents working for the United States during the 1980s. All of the U.S. agents were jailed, and most were executed. Ames was convicted of espionage in 1994 and is serving a life sentence without the possibility of parole. When asked by the *New York Times* about his motivation, Ames replied "Money—money was the motivation.

These other ideas and reasons were only enablers, if you will. I mean, plenty of people need money. A number of people throughout the agency's history have stolen money from the agency and have done terrible things for money." According to a 1994 interview with then-Director of Central Intelligence, R. James Woolsey, Ames betrayed his country because he "wanted a bigger house and a Jaguar."[21]

To be sure, there are many security clearance holders who run into financial difficulties and do not commit espionage for money. In both the Ames and Hanssen cases experts have speculated on the contextual and psychological reasons, in addition to financial gain, that these men committed their crimes. The Defense Personnel and Security Research Center (PERSEREC) lists several traits common to many spies, including antisocial behavior, inability to form commitments, narcissism, impulsiveness, and paranoia.

These examples are just some of the many-faceted threats that the security clearance system is supposed to mitigate. People seeking financial remuneration constitute just one element of that threat. In addition to the psychological factors that must come into play if one is to betray one's country, greed is and will always be a common human frailty.

Crimes of Conscience

In 1967, Daniel Ellsberg had contributed to a top-secret study about the Vietnam War commissioned by the secretary of defense. These documents later became known collectively as the Pentagon Papers; officially titled, *United States–Vietnam Relations, 1945–1967: A Study Prepared by the Department of Defense*, they are a history of U.S. political-military involvement in Vietnam from 1945 to 1967. Ellsberg, who worked for the RAND Corporation, held high-level security clearances and was one of only a few individuals who had access to the complete set of documents. The papers were leaked to the media by Ellsberg, and first brought to the attention of the public on the front page of the *New York Times* in 1971. A 1996 article in that publication said that the Pentagon Papers had demonstrated, among other things, that the Johnson administration had "systematically lied, not only to the public but also to Congress."[22]

But what the Pentagon Papers and Ellsberg also represented to the administration was a new kind of threat. Ellsberg was driven by his own sense of outrage. He wanted the American people to know what their government was doing secretly in their name.

It was not so much the release of the specific information that made Ellsberg such a national security threat to the administration.[23] What bothered the Nixon administration was that Ellsberg had leaked the information to the press. He had been a trusted employee with the highest level of security clearance, and he had betrayed that trust. Not for the benefit of the enemy. Not for money or personal gain. But for his own ideological and ultimately patriotic reasons. Ellsberg was charged with violating the Espionage Act of 1917 and other theft and conspiracy laws; he was subject to a total maximum sentence of 115 years. But owing to government misconduct and illegal evidence gathering, including illegal wiretapping (the FBI had recorded Ellsberg without a court order), and the fact that the Nixon White House was imploding under the Watergate scandal, all charges against Ellsberg were dismissed in May 1973.

Edward Snowden, an American computer specialist and National Security Agency (NSA) contractor, worked for the CIA and NSA before leaking details of several top-secret United States and British government mass-surveillance programs to the press in 2013. The retaliation against Snowden was immediate. The State Department revoked his passport, which left him stranded in Russia where he was granted temporary asylum. His actions spurred considerable and ongoing national and international debate over whether his theft and disclosures of classified information were justified. While the Obama administration called the act treasonous and claimed that great damage was done to national security, others applaud the disclosures because of the amount of government intrusion they revealed. Supporters of Snowden point to the important public discussion he triggered about officials lying to Congress and proper oversight of surveillance programs.[24]

In reference to the oath of allegiance that all federal employees take to defend the U.S. Constitution "against enemies foreign and domestic," Snowden implied in an interview that he had conformed more closely to the intent of the oath than had intelligence officials who were later found to have misrepresented the extent of NSA surveillance programs to Congress. "The oath of allegiance is not an oath of secrecy. . . . That is an oath to the Constitution. That is the oath I kept that [NSA Director] Keith Alexander and [Director of National Intelligence] James Clapper did not."[25]

News stories focus on the government's culpability in recruiting Snowden and giving him the levels of clearance and access they did. Some noted that the government's contracted screening process was questionable."[26] In addition to the faulty investigatory processes eventually revealed in the Snowden case, security professionals at the NSA were not made aware that Snowden's previous CIA bosses had doubts about him. As the *New York Times* reported, "In hindsight, officials said, the report by the C.I.A. supervisor and the agency's suspicions might have been the first serious warnings of the disclosures to come, and the biggest missed opportunity to review Mr. Snowden's top-secret clearance or at least put his future work at the N.S.A. under much greater scrutiny."[27]

True Believers

Ana Belén Montes, a former senior analyst at the Defense Intelligence Agency, was arrested in September 2001 and subsequently charged with conspiracy to commit espionage for the government of Cuba. During the course of the investigation against her, it was determined that Montes had passed classified information to the Cuban government, including the identities of four U.S. spies. In 2002, Montes pleaded guilty to the charge and was sentenced to twenty-five years in prison.[28] According to her lawyer, Montes committed espionage for moral reasons: "She felt the Cubans were treated unfairly by the U.S. government."

Walter Kendall Myers is a retired U.S. State Department officer who, with his wife, Gwendolyn, was arrested and indicted in June 2009 on charges of spying for Cuba for nearly thirty years. According to a law enforcement official interviewed by CNN, "The couple were 'true believers' in the Cuban system."[29]

Mental Illness

In September 2013, Navy contractor and former Navy reservist Aaron Alexis killed twelve people in a shooting rampage inside the Washington DC, Navy Yard. Incensed, Congress called for then–Secretary of Defense Chuck Hagel to reform the security clearance system in order to prevent individuals with personality disorders from obtaining a security clearance. Hagel acknowledged to lawmakers that "a lot of red flags" had been missed in the background investigation of the Navy Yard shooter. Pentagon leaders struggled with whether a string of minor arrests, mental health issues, and other behavioral problems should have been enough to strip him of his security clearance or deny him access to the secure facility in southeast Washington. Hagel ordered a Pentagon review of the physical security and access procedures at all U.S. defense facilities worldwide, as well as a study of the programs used for granting and renewing the security clearances for the military, civilian employees, and contractors, and promised Capitol Hill "where there are gaps, we will close them."[30]

But the cases of Aaron Alexis and Nidal Malik Hasan, a U.S. Army major and psychiatrist who fatally shot thirteen people and injured more than thirty others at Fort Hood, Texas, in 2009, demonstrate how difficult it will be to close the gaps in the personnel security clearance process by observing and identifying red flags surrounding mental health issues and granting and maintaining security clearances.

While the Department of Defense claims to have "developed and validated an assessment instrument that efficiently assesses dysfunctional aspects of personality,"[31] and such an instrument may have been used to develop the profiles related to the Obama administration's new insider threat policies, those types of ambitious assessments did not come into play at the Navy Yard and Fort Hood incidents.

Wiki-Leaking

Chelsea Elizabeth Manning, a U.S. Army intelligence analyst, was convicted in July 2013 of violations of the Espionage Act and other offenses after releasing 250,000 U.S. diplomatic cables and 500,000 Army cables to WikiLeaks and was sentenced to thirty-five years in prison.[32] During the trial, the media sensationalized Manning's transgender identity, airing a photo, released by the Pentagon, of Manning wearing a wig and lipstick. But there were real issues plaguing Manning that may have flagged her as a security risk. For example, before her arrest, a supervisor sent a memo to her unit's behavioral psychologists noting that Manning's "instability was a constant source of concern" and that it included "frequent catatonic periods," such as when she stopped talking and went blank in the midst of a briefing. Manning's own explanation for leaking the documents as expressed in an email to WikiLeaks was "removing the fog of war and revealing the true nature of 21st century asymmetric warfare."[33]

Whistleblowers

Both Snowden and Manning consider themselves whistleblowers. They contend that the information they leaked contributes to a more informed dialogue on U.S. national security issues. The U.S. government does not agree, so the protections in place for whistleblowers do not apply to them. But the government does acknowledge that there are times when whistleblowers do and will need protection from retaliation for exposing government activities.

U.S. Presidential Policy Directive 19, signed by President Obama, is designed to ensure that employees who serve in the intelligence community or have access to classified information can effectively report waste, fraud, and abuse while protecting classified information. It is the executive order establishing standards for all federal agencies with employees covered by the directive, including those under Defense Intelligence Community Whistleblower Protection and the U.S. Department of Defense Whistleblower Program. It also prohibits retaliation against these employees for their reports.[34] But the Policy Directive does not do enough, although it does represent a significant breakthrough, according to Government Accountability Project legal director Tom Devine. He worries that government employees who embarrass their bosses will still face retaliation, and that the fox has been left to guard the proverbial henhouse: "Regulations to enforce whistleblower rights will be written by the same agencies that routinely are the defendants in whistleblower retaliation lawsuits. . . . it is no substitute for Congress to legislate permanent rights for national security whistleblowers, with third-party enforcement the same as for other employees."[35] So even though the government pays lip service to protecting national security employees from retaliation, as we will see in the following chapters, it still doesn't really do it.

The Insider Threat

Even before Edward Snowden exposed the NSA's secret collection programs, the Obama administration was designing a new personnel security clearance policy to help identify what was fast becoming a priority for national security—the insider threat. Part of the administration's new policy guidance now requires federal employees to observe and report on each other. On November 21, 2012, President Obama issued the White House memorandum "National Insider Threat Policy and Minimum Standards for Executive Branch Insider Threat Programs." The policy broadens the reach of anticipated security risks from just the national security bureaucracies to most federal departments and agencies, including the Peace Corps, the Social Security Administration, and the Education and Agriculture Departments. It emphasizes leaks of classified material, but catchall definitions of "insider threat" give agencies latitude to pursue and penalize a range of other conduct.[36]

To help federal employees identify "high-risk" individuals, the Defense Information Systems Agency (DISA) created a "Cyber-Awareness Challenge." One section of the security challenge requires employees to identify the threat level of hypothetical individuals they encounter in their offices. It offers an example of a high-threat individual: an Indian woman named Hema, who travels to India twice a year to visit family and who "speaks openly of unhappiness with U.S. foreign policy." This woman demonstrates an "adequate work quality" and has had her car repossessed. "Based on her statements, this employee demonstrates divided loyalty," the program explains. "Paired with her financial difficulties and foreign travel, she is a high threat."[37]

On July 31, 2013, the secretary of the Army formally established its Insider Threat Program. The program "will ensure the security and safety of Army computer networks by establishing an integrated capability to monitor and audit user activity across all domains to detect and mitigate activity indicative of insider threat behavior," wrote Army Secretary John M. McHugh in Army Directive 2013–18.

Naturally, coming on the heels of the Manning WikiLeaks experience, there is much in the directive about monitoring employees' computer activities. In addition, the directive mandates that the Army "develop a capability to vet personnel for access to Army facilities against authoritative U.S. Government databases to identify potential criminals, terrorists or other security and insider threats." There are also some unexpected new requirements. For example, for the first time, information will be gleaned from medical sources, "The Surgeon General will provide information from medical sources, consistent with privacy laws and regulations, to authorized personnel to help them recognize the presence of an insider threat."[38]

President Obama and the Espionage Act

The U.S. Department of Justice has charged Edward Snowden with three felonies, including two under the Espionage Act. The Obama administration has been particularly keen to use the Espionage Act as a tool against leakers: "Prior to Barack Obama's inauguration, there were a grand total of three prosecutions of leakers under the Espionage Act (including the prosecution of Daniel Ellsberg by the Nixon DOJ). . . . But during the Obama presidency, there are now seven such prosecutions: more than double the number under all prior U.S. presidents combined."[39]

Those charged under the Espionage Act during the Obama administration include NSA employee Thomas Drake, who was charged with retaining classified documents for "unauthorized disclosure"; Shamai Leibowitz, a linguist and translator for the FBI, who pleaded guilty to leaking classified information to a blogger; Stephen Kim, an analyst working under contract with the State

Department, who was indicted for giving classified information to Fox News about North Korea; Jeffery Sterling, a CIA officer, who was charged with leaking information about the CIA's efforts against Iran's nuclear program; and John Kiriakou, who was charged with leaking information about the interrogation of an Al Qaeda leader and disclosing the name of a CIA analyst involved.[40]

I present some of the evolution of national security threats reflected in policies that impact government workers because by looking at the history of national security priorities, we are able to identify moments of crisis when the national security bureaucracy tends to outgrow its legitimate need and the dynamic by which prudent security measures give way to imprudent paranoia. Given the multifaceted nature of the many and varied types of threats against which the system is supposed to protect, one wonders if any one set of technologies or tools can do the job and we can see why the system so often fails. Indeed, the system designed to predict such threats has proven faulty in many ways. One of its worst faults is the way the system is wrongly used against employees who, rather than presenting an actual threat, merely embarrass their bosses by exposing fraud, waste, abuse, or other whistleblowing activities.

Let us now move on and consider how the system is designed to work, and some of the many reasons why it often doesn't.

2   The Personnel Security
Clearance Process

It has been said that "journalism is the first rough draft of history."[1] Good journalists are smart, curious, and relentless in seeking the latest and most relevant information surrounding their beats. So to flesh out some of the controversies surrounding the clearance process, I rely on news reports. I adopted this technique from my father, Irwin Deutscher, an eminent sociologist who described journalists as "research assistants" because they share many of the traits of scientists and academics. He says that, "Like scientists, contemporary newspaper reporters are trained to exercise a degree of detachment, value objectivity, check the reliability of sources, and confirm their discoveries with outside evidence. Both scientists and journalists are subject to scrutiny by their peers and to both internal and external sanctions should their integrity be questioned. In a real sense the careers of both are contingent upon the maintenance of credibility."[2]

Sharing my father's opinion, I feel journalists provide useful context for some of the debate surrounding the personnel security clearance process. I have tried to choose the most reliable sources.

Going through the Process

According to the U.S. General Accounting Office, approximately 900,000 security clearances are processed annually by the government, with the majority for defense-related agencies and intelligence community (IC) positions.

The apparatus that sustains the national personnel security clearance process is a vast web of people, institutions, policies, and processes designed to vet and monitor applicants who seek to serve the nation. The tools and methodologies employed in the process are a mix of science, art, and human ingenuity. An individual cannot request or obtain a security clearance on his or her own. First, one must be selected or hired for a position (either as a federal employee or as a contracted worker for a commercial firm with a government contract) that requires a clearance. Only then can an agency, employer, or sponsor submit an application for a clearance. A security clearance, unlike a driver's license, is assigned not to an individual per se, but rather to a national security position. Specifically, clearance is granted to a position with a "need to know" certain secrets.[3]

As I outlined in the previous chapter, the personnel security clearance system has a long history. But it was Executive Order 12968, signed by President Clinton in 1995, that established the uniform policies for the assignment and administration of personnel security clearances and access to classified information that remain in effect today. The order details eligibility requirements and administrative procedures for granting or denying access and for appealing such determinations. The order describes characteristics the government wants in individuals seeking clearance (such as honesty, reliability, and discretion), and it describes characteristics that it seeks to avoid (conflicting allegiances and potential for coercion). It also stipulates that if there is ever any doubt about an individual's trustworthiness, the individual must be denied clearance on the grounds of national security. The order dictates that "eligibility for access to classified information shall be granted only to employees who are United States citizens for whom an appropriate investigation has been completed and whose personal and professional history affirmatively indicates loyalty to the United States, strength of character, trustworthiness, honesty, reliability, discretion, and sound judgment, as well as freedom from conflicting allegiances and potential for coercion, and willingness and ability to abide by regulations governing the use, handling, and protection of classified information."[4]

The Background Investigation

The "appropriate investigation" required by the executive order for most prospective federal employees seeking cleared jobs includes completing forms (which at a minimum may include the Standard Form 86 (SF-86) and the Questionnaire for National Security Positions) that applicants must sign authorizing release of any and all information to Security Clearance Investigators, including records as detailed below. Databases will be searched, including the Security/ Suitability Investigations Index, Defense Clearance and Investigations Index, fingerprint classification, and the Federal Bureau of Investigation's investigative index. A credit check will be conducted covering all residences, employment, and education.

The background investigation begins after an individual has been given a conditional offer of employment and has completed the required forms. The SF-86 contains a statement that applicants must sign authorizing release of information to investigators, including sealed records, juvenile records, expunged records, and medical records. According to the State Department's website:

> Once the security package is received by the Office of Personnel Security and Suitability, it will be reviewed for completeness, and the information will be formally entered into a case management system. National agency record checks and scanned fingerprint checks are then conducted. A case manager will direct the background investigation to cover key events and contacts from the individual's past and present history.

> A critical step in the background investigation is the face-to-face interview the individual will have with a DS investigator. This interview usually occurs within a few weeks of an individual submitting a complete security clearance package.

> DS investigators are located in the United States and overseas. These investigators verify the information an individual has

supplied in his or her security package, such as where he or she has lived, gone to school, and worked. Investigators talk to current and former neighbors, supervisors, co-workers, classmates, as well as to the references an individual provided. Investigators also contact law enforcement agencies in each of the places an individual has lived, worked, or attended school."[5]

Once the investigators have completed a report, adjudicators weigh the results against existing guidelines for security clearances. In addition to the background investigation, other tests or procedures may be required, such as a urinalysis or a polygraph examination. After the investigation, most individuals are granted a security clearance, although complicating factors or derogatory findings may delay a decision or result in a denial. And as I discuss later, some investigators have been negligent or dishonest.

PROBLEMS WITH THE INVESTIGATIVE PROCESS:
THE INVESTIGATIVE BACKLOG

Sometimes efforts by the government to fix one problem can result in a new one. This may have been the case when, in the wake of the September 11, 2001, terrorist attacks in the United States, increased demand for cleared workers resulted in a backlog in the investigation process that motivated Congress to intervene to improve the way agencies vetted cleared workers. As the Center for Public Policy observed at the time, the investigative process was not then sufficient to handle the burgeoning investigative caseload, and:

> Soon after its hiring binge began, the government's ambitions collided with a creaky system for conducting the background checks needed to approve job applicants for security clearances. By 2004, the backlog of contractors awaiting approval had reached the size of a small city: at least 188,000. Complaints by federal agencies and job-seekers alike grew so intense that lawmakers became fixated on finding a solution. Additional personnel were added to the federal investigations process, but Washington largely chose a different path that promised to be cheaper and quicker—shortening the time allowed for the reviews, by law."[6]

In 2004, Congress passed the Intelligence Reform and Terrorism Prevention Act (IRTPA), which required that by 2009 agencies must process 90 percent of clearance applications within an average of sixty days.[7] Because of the new mandate, many agencies chose to farm the bulk of the investigative work out to contractors and thus created a whole new issue. Agencies relied in particular on U.S. Investigations Services (USIS), which later came under scrutiny in 2013 when it was discovered that the company had conducted the security clearance investigation for NSA leaker Edward Snowden. Though certainly the most splashy instance of failure, the *Miami Herald* reported that the U.S. Office of Personnel Management confirmed an investigation of USIS was under way even before the Snowden incident brought the company to public attention. The inspectors general were informed of fraudulent cases by whistleblowers and former investigators, finding that "background investigators reported interviews that never occurred, recorded answers to questions that were never asked, and documented records checks that were never conducted. . . . One contractor faked 1,600 credit checks. As it turned out, her own background investigation had been faked by a background investigator in a separate case."[8]

Urinalysis

In 1986, President Reagan issued Executive Order 12564, The Drug Free Federal Workplace, which established random drug testing for civil service employees. So today, urine testing for drug use is part of the screening process for security clearance holders.

But in 1974, Department of Defense (DoD) Instruction 1010.1 had already been issued establishing random testing of all eligible members of the armed forces who had been on active duty for more than thirty days.[9] In 2001, the American Forces Press Service reported that DoD labs test 60,000 urine samples each month, and all active duty members must undergo a urinalysis at least once a year.[10]

According to the Department of Defense Inspector General's Office, "once an applicant is notified that they must take the drug test, they have 48 hours from the time of notification to complete the test. If the test is not completed within the 48 hours, the tentative offer of employment is revoked, and the applicant must reapply for any future OIG positions."[11]

According to the Department of Labor, Office of the Assistant Secretary for Policy, the forty-eight-hour rule is standard.[12] Yet in my experience at the Department of Defense, I was given only a few hours' notice before testing. For example, I would get an email at my office in the morning requiring me to report to a clinic in the Pentagon that same day. Typically, after showing proper government identification, one is guided to a toilet stall and instructed to urinate into a plastic cup. According to the Navy Drug Screening Laboratory, "The employee's urine is collected in a specially designed secure cup, sealed with tamper-resistant tape. The individual is then required to initial the sample and it is sent to a testing laboratory to be screened for drugs. At the collection site, the urine sample begins to go through a specified 'chain of custody' to ensure that it is not tampered with or invalidated through lab or employee error."[13]

But no matter how controlled its scientific implementation, just as with other personnel clearance screening methodologies, the urinalysis is not perfect. And it is not without its critics. Mathew Tully notes that most service members don't imagine that they could test positive. But innocent people do test positive, just as drug users sometimes test negative.[14] In an article for the *Army Times*, Tully observes that "many commanders want to believe only drug users test positive on unit urinalysis. This is simply untrue." He points to the commercial products designed to remove traces of drugs from urine, allowing tests of drug users to appear negative, and goes on to describe how an Army captain who had never used drugs tested positive.[15]

> This young captain had a family from South America who had come to the U.S. for a visit. One of the gifts his grandmother brought him was . . . tea. . . . Could the tea bags have caused this captain to test positive for cocaine? Of course, the command was not buying that story and pushed for a court-martial—until two independent drug testing firms hired by council pointed to the fact that several ingredients in mate de coca tea bags could

cause a urinalysis to read high levels of benzoylecgonine. BZE is the metabolite of cocaine. Upon receiving the reports, the command agreed to drop all charges against the captain and reinstate him into command. Many people in the military still believe it is not possible to innocently test positive on a urinalysis. But a urinalysis is not 100 percent accurate, and assorted other issues cause these tests to come back improperly positive and negative.[16]

Executive Order 12564 instituted mandatory drug testing for all civil service employees with a security clearance. In 2012 the policy was expanded to include abuse of prescription drugs as well as illegal drugs.

The Polygraph Exam

A polygraph examination uses a machine that is designed to measure physiological indicators such as blood pressure, pulse, and respiration, while asking the subject a series of questions. Proponents argue that, when conducted by a competent and experienced polygraph examiner, deceptive answers will produce physiological responses that can be differentiated from those associated with truthful answers. According to Polygraph Investigative Services, a company that performs polygraph examinations for federal government clients:

> Polygraph theory is based on the psychophysiological principle. Psychophysiology is the branch of psychology that is concerned with the physiological bases of psychological processes. The assumption of polygraph examiners is that during the testing phase, and according to the psychophysiological principle, when the subject hears a question in response to which he or she intends to lie, the brain triggers automatic and uncontrollable physiological changes captured by the machine. These changes are recorded by the examiner.[17]

Typically, there are two areas in which the polygraph is used. The first is in a criminal context, the "did you do it?" examination in which questions surrounding a specific incident or crime are asked. In this context, according to researchers at the Department of Defense National Center for Credibility Assessment (NCCA), the machine has demonstrated some accuracy.[18] The other major use of the polygraph is in the screening that takes place during the personnel security clearance process. NCCA researchers concede that it is difficult to measure effectiveness in this context. Nevertheless, there are currently twenty-eight federal programs using the polygraph to screen for clearances, including the Departments of Homeland Security, Energy, State, Treasury, and Justice and the Central Intelligence Agency.

The NCCA (formerly the Department of Defense Polygraph Institute) at the U.S. Army Training Center in Fort Jackson, South Carolina is the federally funded institution providing graduate and continuing education courses in a discipline called "Psychophysiological Detection of Deception" (PDD). The NCCA also offers graduate-level coursework in how to administer and analyze polygraph tests.

As administered by the Army, usually the polygraph examination consists of three phases. The examiner begins by reviewing the security package (which includes the SF-86, finger prints, investigative findings and other information collected during the application process) on the individual (the subject). During the pretest phase, the examiner discusses with the subject how the test will be conducted and reviews the test questions that will be asked during the test. The testing phase consists of a series of tests that record the subject's physiological responses as the subject answers the set of questions. After the test, the examiner reviews all of the test data obtained and interprets the polygraph charts. Then the examiner reaches one of three conclusions: that the subject is telling the truth, that the subject is not telling the truth, or that the results are inconclusive. At that point the examiner submits a report to the hiring agency that consists of a synopsis of the case information, a list of the test questions, the subject's answers, and the examiner's opinion about the subject's truthfulness or deception.[19]

The examiner may or may not share the findings with the applicant. The tests are, however, uploaded into a massive database—the Investigative Records Repository (IRR), also referred to as the

"Improved" Investigative Records Repository (iIRR)—maintained by the Department of Defense.

The process used to screen border guards for a security clearance, as administered by the Department of Homeland Security, Customs and Border Protection, is detailed by Andrew Becker of the Center for Investigative Reporting, who touches on another objective of the process, the confession or "cleansing." Becker reports that, for the test:

> Polygraphers ask law enforcement applicants questions in two categories: suitability and national security. The suitability questions probe illegal drug use, involvement with serious crimes and falsification of a job application. National security questions seek answers related to espionage, unauthorized contact with foreigners and the mishandling of classified information. . . . Finally, there is a post-test interview, if need be, when the polygrapher encourages applicants to "cleanse" themselves. . . . Examiners delve deeper into certain responses during the post-test, downplaying any transgressions while emphasizing the need for honesty. The overall process typically runs three or four hours, but can go longer if the applicant continues to admit things.[20]

The data collected during the exam (scrolls of paper that visually record, retain, and exhibit the subject's reactions to questions) is used by the individual examiner, sometimes in consultation with the examiner's colleagues or boss, to make a final determination of credibility. The decision of the examiner (the polygrapher and senior polygrapher) is final in most cases.

Yet, according to the National Research Council, thousands of people a year could be identified as lying in polygraph screenings when they are not. And under the current system, many of them have no way to legally challenge a polygrapher's conclusion. In some exceptional cases polygraph results have been appealed. But an appeal requires a lengthy and expensive legal battle that most applicants are not in a position to pursue.

One exception was reported by McClatchy Newspapers when Michael Pillsbury, a contracted consultant, had to fight claims by CIA polygraphers that he had admitted leaking sensitive information.

Two things worked in his favor: He had the money for good lawyers, and he was not a federal employee. Unlike federal employees, as a contractor he was permitted to dispute the CIA's polygraph determination through the Defense Office of Hearings and Appeals: "Despite the CIA's insistence he couldn't appeal outside the agency, he discovered that as a government consultant he could turn to an obscure board of administrative judges. After an almost two-year dispute . . . he was able to rebut the statements attributed to him and a judge granted him the top-secret access requested. The board, the Defense Office of Hearings and Appeals, is mainly set up for contractors and consultants, but even those who fall into those categories often discover they're barred for other reasons."[21]

According to a McClatchy Newspapers investigation, the Department of Defense conducts approximately 46,000 national security polygraphs each year.[22] And the use of the machine for security clearance screening is still on the rise. Often when federal employees are required to submit to a polygraph examination for federal employment or to keep a federal job, they do so unwillingly. According to Katie Howard at Federal News Radio, "It's incredible the things that people will then say and admit to. And once they have admitted to things that are problematic, then the agency will use the person's own words to screen them away from having a job."[23]

It is not surprising to learn that such confessions are obtained during the polygraph exams in light of how the NCCA's Psychophysiological Detection of Deception (PDD) Program trains polygraph examiners. The course description for PDD 501, "Interview Techniques," states that "interviewing skills facilitate and complement the PDD process . . . students are taught how to encourage self-report of behaviors relevant to the test issues."[24]

But part of the problem with the polygraph program is that it may be overstepping the bounds of what is "relevant" to national security. Katie Howard, reporting for Federal News Radio, notes that in their quest to encourage self-reporting of relevant behaviors, some polygraph examiners can delve into "a lot of serious things that are pretty personal and might be viewed . . . as maybe across the line."[25] The Employee Polygraph Protection Act of 1988 (EPPA) prohibits private employers from using polygraph testing to screen applicants on the following subjects: religious beliefs or affiliations (unless specifically relevant to the job); beliefs or opinions regarding racial matters (except to the extent that any such biases could interfere with one's ability to fairly and objectively perform his or her job); political beliefs or affiliations; beliefs, affiliations or lawful activities regarding unions or labor organizations or lawful sexual preferences or activities."[26] However, that legislation does not apply to federal agencies. And indeed government polygraph examiners have crossed that line and even government-mandated norms when it comes to intrusive questioning. They continue to do so according to a McClatchy Newspapers review of documents at the National Reconnaissance Office (NRO), which included internal policy documents, memos and agency emails, and interviews with dozens of polygraphers and national security experts. The news service found that NRO was pushing "ethical and possibly legal limits" by establishing a system to track the number of confessions obtained by polygraphers that were then used to determine annual performance bonuses. McClatchy found that annual performance reviews were bolstered by "summoning employees and job applicants for multiple polygraph tests to ask about a wide array of personal behavior. In some cases, polygraph examiners were found to have altered test results in what some polygraphers say is an effort to justify more probing of employees' and applicants' private lives. The disclosures by employees and applicants include a wide range of behavior and private thoughts such as drug use, child abuse, suicide attempts, depression and sexual deviancy." The McClatchy findings prompted a congressional investigation of NRO's polygraph program, during which "Sen. Charles Grassley (R-Iowa) instructed the Department of Defense to investigate whether the NRO had overstepped its bounds," explaining that "the polygraphers should have clear rules and regulations about the topics they can and should cover in their work."[27]

As NCCA's course number PDD 504, "Methods I," poignantly explains, there is a history here of bureaucrats becoming overzealous. The 2013 course catalog stated that curriculum covered "the historical aspects of PDD beginning with the methods of detecting deception during the [Spanish] Inquisition to the modern approaches of the present day." The language for the current course description has been softened a little, to "methods of detecting deception in ancient history to the scientifically founded approaches of the present."[28] But you get the idea. Bureaucrats with that kind of power might tend to overstep.

In 2002 the National Academy of Sciences declared polygraph examinations dangerously unreliable and urged the federal government to cease depending on them to screen for security risks. The study found that the polygraph not only incorrectly deems large numbers of people who are telling the truth to be liars, but may have allowed spies and others posing security risks into sensitive positions because they were able to pass their polygraph tests. For example, Aldrich Ames passed two polygraph tests while spying for the Soviet Union.[29]

"National security is too important to be left to such a blunt instrument," according to Stephen Fienberg, the chairman of the National Academy of Sciences panel that conducted the study. The panel called the current technology badly outdated, and recommended the government pursue research into prospective new lie-detection techniques, while noting that such techniques have been illusive to date, "It may also be that research has not yet identified the most valid behavioral indicators of deception."[30]

And some at the Department of Defense's National Center for Credibility Assessment agree with that recommendation. I conducted a telephone interview with a professor at the NCCA who said as much: "The problem is that we've been using the same single diagnostic tool for decades."

In spite of the National Academy of Sciences' recommendations to improve the technology and the government's promise to do so, there appear to have been few modifications to the polygraph since the original U.S. Army Polygraph School was established in 1951.

FAILING THE POLYGRAPH

Whether reliable or not, there is little doubt that the polygraph has ruined some careers. It has also prevented some from pursuing careers in federal service. It has turned some applicants sour on the agencies to which they have applied. This story comes from a blog for federal employees:

> During my polygraph, I was told I failed the test . . . what has continued to bother me is the fact that the FBI can tell an applicant that he/she failed the polygraph and not have to show any proof that they (FBI) are not lying. I requested a retest, but the FBI declined. . . . However, they were content to call me a "liar" and send me on my way. I have lost all respect for the FBI as an institution, and even though I love this country and everything it stands for, I have no use for the FBI . . . . If people like this, who will call you a liar without any proof, are charged with protecting our country, God help us all.[31]

EXPERIENCING TECHNICAL DIFFICULTIES

In light of the polygraph's scientifically dubious reputation and its susceptibility to abuse, it is even more alarming to learn that the equipment examiners rely on to make their clearance determinations does not work as well as it should. Marisa Taylor found that a particular brand of polygraph instrument used by the FBI and other federal agencies, the LX4000, manufactured by the Lafayette Instrument Company of North Lafayette, Indiana, is not working as hoped. She reports that polygraphers have documented problems with the measurement of sweat by the LX4000 and that often the sweat measurement is seen as especially indicative of deception, yet "The manufacturer of the LX4000, Lafayette Instrument Co. Inc., describes the problem as rare but it isn't able to specify what that means." Lest they be singled out as the only company making defective polygraph devices, the Lafayette Company provided Taylor with a statement noting that other polygraphs use the same technology: "The potential for occasional differences to be observed was already clearly described in the published literature, not limited to the Lafayette polygraph system, and anecdotal experience confirms it is an occasional occurrence."[32]

Taylor contends that the FBI polygraphs approximately 13,000 people a year for initial security clearances and that, "According to records, the bureau has at least a 30 percent failure rate in its job screening. As many as 40 percent of special agent applicants don't get the job because of their polygraph test results." Federal agencies continue to use the device even though it has proven to be defective (at least sometimes). For example, in August 2008, after the McClatchy story broke, the Defense Intelligence Agency, which also uses the Lafayette polygraph systems LX4000 for routine testing, announced that "though they are aware of the problems with the machine . . . it would subject each of its 5,700 prospective and current employees to polygraph testing at least once annually."[33]

BEATING "THE BOX"

Another problem with the polygraph, according to critics and advocates alike, is that, even when calibrated properly, individuals can manipulate the technology by learning how to control bodily functions (nervousness, heart rate, sweat, breathing rate) that would trigger responses and give polygraphers pause to further investigate and interrogate test takers. David Lykken, a behavioral geneticist known for his work on lie detection, tells how he once helped an individual pass a polygraph. "The only hard part was learning how to keep a straight face," he later told Mr. Lykken.[34]

During the Obama administration, those who counseled individuals on passing a polygraph test were considered threats to national security. According to Taylor, the pursuit and criminal treatment of polygraph coaches is a result of the Obama administration's overreach in the aftermath of insider leaks from individuals such as Chelsea Manning and Edward Snowden.

To defend against those who would "beat the box," the NCCA is ready. PDD course number 505, "PDD Methods," provides students with countermeasures for countering countermeasures: "This course acquaints the student . . . examiner to the various types of mental, physical, and pharmacological countermeasures that might be encountered in PDD testing and provides counter-countermeasures an examiner might utilize to neutralize these countermeasures."[35]

Personnel Security and Big Data: The IT Systems

In 2008, then-President George W. Bush asked his Cabinet for proposals on how to make personnel security clearance decisions more quickly, effectively, and efficiently. In April of that year, the Joint Security and Suitability Reform Team delivered a plan of action for streamlining security clearance processes governmentwide. Among other things, the team recommended that automation be used to make the process faster and "that continuous evaluation techniques replace periodic investigation, using more frequent automated database checks to identify security relevant issues."[36]

The Department of Defense was already maintaining several automated databases that they were using for security clearance adjudication and administration. Based on the team's recommendations, in January 2009 the deputy secretary of defense directed the transfer of existing Department of Defense enterprisewide IT systems associated with personnel security clearances from the Defense Security Service to the Defense Manpower Data Center (DMDC). The applications that transferred from DSS to DMDC included: the Joint Personnel Adjudication System (JPAS), the Defense Central Index of Investigations (DCII), the Secure Web Fingerprint Transmission (SWFT), and the Investigative Records Repository (IRR) (also referred to as the "Improved" Investigative Records Repository (iIRR). The program management and operational responsibilities of these four transitioned applications would now fall under the Personnel Security/Assurance (PSA) Division, which is a component of the Identity Management Directorate at DMDC.[37]

According to the Department of Defense Personnel and Research Center (PERSEREC), changing technology has had a major impact on the way personnel security adjudicators do their work. The expectation, as with all technological inventions, is that the systems will deliver valuable services while saving time and money.[38] When an applicant enters into the national personnel security clearance system by applying for a federal job that requires clearance, the individual's application forms and all of the data resulting from the investigation and testing processes are entered into these databases.

The Defense Central Index of Investigations (DCII) System is an automated central index that identifies investigations conducted by DoD investigative agencies and personnel security determinations made by DoD adjudicative authorities. Access to DCII is normally limited to the Department of Defense and other federal agencies that have adjudicative, investigative, and/or counterintelligence missions.[39] The Secure Web Fingerprint Transmission (SWFT) program enables cleared defense industry users to submit electronic fingerprints (e-fingerprints) and demographic information for applicants who require an investigation by the Office of Personnel Management (OPM) for a personnel security clearance.[40]

According to PERSEREC, the Automated Continuing Evaluation System (ACES) was developed as an automated approach to assessing eligibility for access to classified information in between an initial background investigation and a periodic reinvestigation (PR). It is also to be used "during the career of a cleared employee, in between PRs." PERSEREC, aware of the Obama administration's focus on insider threats, hopes that ACES will help to solve that problem too: "With regard to response to the insider threat, when fully operational, ACES will offer to the DoD earlier detection and intervention and an increased range of issues for determining vulnerabilities."[41]

But there is cause for concern in the trend toward increased dependence on technology. Storing so much sensitive information in government databases has its downside, as demonstrated during a massive hack of the ACES system in 2015 in which all of the stolen information was from background investigations used for evaluating security clearances. "The team has now concluded with high confidence that sensitive information, including the Social Security numbers (SSNs) of 21.5 million individuals, was stolen from the background investigation databases," OPM wrote in a statement. "This includes 19.7 million individuals that applied for a background investigation, and 1.8 million non-applicants, predominantly spouses or co-habitants of applicants."[42]

There is also reason to worry about the focus and claims of massive information technology systems on cost- and time-cutting measures. We have already seen what those parameters have wrought in the wake of legislation specifying timeliness for clearances—remember that fraudulent investigations were one result. Part of the purpose of the increased use of technology in the clearance system appears to be to remove some of the human element in the current decision-making process. But it may be wise to question that aim.

Marko Hakamaa, a former background investigator for OPM, writing for ClearanceJobs.com, describes the job that human adjudicators perform in the personnel security clearance process, noting that all agencies have requirements that must be met by those assigned as adjudicators before they are allowed to review background investigations and make adjudicative determinations. Among those requirements are that adjudicators themselves undergo either a background investigation (BI) or a single-scope background investigation (SSBI) and are required to have completed specific training courses. In addition, Hakamaa notes that "new adjudicators or those with less experience have senior adjudicators there to train, mentor, provide oversight, and to ensure the determinations made are sound and fall within established guidelines. For the more experienced adjudicators, refresher training is completed in order to stay current with ever-changing security mandates and guidance."[43]

One could argue that many adjudication tasks seem inherently human. For example, it is difficult for an automated system to determine the amount of pressure, coercion, exploitation, or duress an individual was under when making certain decisions. And for government workers, there is a lot riding on those determinations. It is hard to build an algorithm that makes determinations about individual contexts and characteristics. It would be easier to build one that uses a cookie-cutter approach.

The Adjudication Decision Support (ADS) System is part of the cookie-cutter approach to removing the human element from the personnel security clearance process. According to PERSEREC, the ADS system can reliably process the electronic results of personnel security investigations and eliminate the need for human adjudicative review of investigations that contain acceptably minor adverse information. It claims that the system is currently saving the government, industry, and taxpayers millions of dollars and substantially expediting the process of clearance applications. PERSEREC anticipates that "approximately 50% of all personnel security and suitability investigations may eventually be eligible for expedited approval by an ADS system."[44]

In the wake of violent workplace incidents instigated by clearance holders, like the Fort Hood and Navy Yard shootings, the Department of Defense has developed and is evaluating an instrument that "assesses dysfunctional aspects of personality that are neither accessible via self-report nor readily observable by others in order to mitigate security, safety and reliability risks associated with personality disorders." But even the Defense Department's PERSEREC acknowledges that this undertaking is not without difficulties, "Security and safety problems are sometimes caused by individuals with particular personality disorders. Identifying such individuals is difficult because: (1) traditional clinical personality assessment methods have diagnostic weaknesses, and (2) there is insufficient information on which personality disorders relate to the greatest security, safety and reliability risks." It is important to note that while PERSEREC understands that "clinical personality assessment methods have flaws," it built the new DIRE/WSAP scale using "a validated and recognized personality assessment instrument—the Shedler-Western Assessment Procedure." It makes no mention of having mitigated the impact of flaws in the assessment, so presumably the flaws noted are also built into the new system.[45]

Among the problems inherent in such a system is the fact that humans must implement it. Certainly, an improved ability "to assess important aspects of employees' mental fitness" would have been useful in September 2013 when a Navy contractor with a personality disorder killed twelve people at the Washington Navy Yard. Lawmakers, after the incident, called for the secretary of defense at the time, Chuck Hagel, to reform the security clearance system to prevent individuals with personality disorders from obtaining and maintaining a clearance. But technological answers would likely have been limited in helping to detect the threat. As Jack Gillum and Eric Tucker reported at the time:

Even with complete data and all of PERSEREC's proposed technological interactivity, the databases would have missed a police report describing [Navy contractor] Alexis as complaining about voices wanting to harm him. There was no arrest made and Alexis was not charged with any wrongdoing. So he wouldn't have been entered into a database at that time. When he called police and told them he couldn't get away from the voices . . . local police did alert officials at the Newport Naval Station about being called to the naval defense contractor's hotel room. But officers didn't hear from them again.[46]

So in this example, the automated systems currently in use did not collect all of the relevant information about an individual. Contrary to any aims to remove human judgment from the process IT systems rely on humans to identify, register, and enter relevant data. Databases may contain important information, but if humans don't know how, when, or if to retrieve and analyze it, it remains useless.

What should have been done with the information that Alexis was hearing voices? Given that information, some security officers could have filed an "incident report" in JPAS that would have triggered an investigation, but other security professionals may not have deemed that information significant enough to document in JPAS. I have noted that adjudicators enter a gray area when making clearance determinations. So in addition to the new big-data solutions to security clearance concerns, there must be appropriate human protocols and practices in place to make the best use of them. So far, such practices do not exist.

While PERSEREC is working on its personality assessment tools, some point to the fact that identifying violent personality disorders was not an original mandate of the personnel security clearance system. This bolsters my assertion that the system must learn to adapt to an indeterminable number of emergent threats while working to improve its current practices. As Gillum and Tucker note:

The government's sprawling system of background checks and security clearances is so unreliable it's virtually impossible to adequately investigate the nearly 5 million Americans who have them and make sure they can be trusted with access to military and sensitive civilian buildings. . . . Case after case has exposed problems for years, including recent instances when workers the government approved have been implicated in mass shootings, espionage and damaging disclosures of national secrets. . . . The system focuses on identifying applicants who could be black-mailed or persuaded to sell national secrets, not commit acts of violence.[47]

Incidents like the Navy Yard shooting demonstrate failures on the part of existing information technology to obtain and flag security data that might help prevent such tragedies. They also show how important it is for individuals tasked with maintaining the personnel security clearance system to make full use of the automated systems available to them.

Another possibility is to monitor personnel with security clearances through social media. According to PERSEREC, "Cybervetting can be defined as checking blogs, social media sites, and other Internet-based sources to identify issues of security concern applicable to people holding or seeking positions of trust." In addition to cybervetting, PERSEREC is pursuing a series of "CyberPsychology studies exploring how certain types of activities in cyber environments . . . can spill over into negative effects on workplace reliability, judgment, and other areas of personnel security concern."[48]

Such studies may be a reaction to critics' contention that Edward Snowden exhibited antigovernment sentiments during online chat sessions, and that Fort Hood shooter Nidal Malik Hasan was in email contact with a Yemen-based imam who was under surveillance by a Joint Terrorism Task Force and monitored by the NSA as a security threat. The cybervetting and cyberpsychology efforts underway at PERSEREC touch on many of the surveillance and privacy issues triggered by Snowden's disclosure of NSA collections that continue to fuel debate about government collection of individual electronic, telephonic, and other habits.

Incident Reporting

So far I have described some of the processes, existing and possible, by which individuals are or could be screened in order to obtain a security clearance. But clearance must also be maintained. Periodic reinvestigations—at a minimum of every five years for top secret, ten years for secret, and fifteen years for confidential—are one way that clearances are maintained, or in some cases revoked.[49]

But when intermittent issues arise with respect to one's existing security clearance they should also be reported. Each such report is placed in the Joint Personnel Adjudication System (JPAS). This type of reporting is generally referred to as an "incident report." An incident may be self-reported; for example, employees are instructed to inform their security office when they receive a traffic violation such as a speeding ticket or a citation for driving while under the influence of alcohol (DWI). Reports can also be made by third parties. Colleagues and coworkers may anonymously report individuals they observe to be impaired by substance or alcohol abuse on or off the job. Coworkers may also report someone for threatening violence or manifesting violent behavior in or outside the workplace. An incident report can come from virtually anywhere.

When an incident is reported, an agency's personnel security officer, usually in consultation with the individual's supervisors, may decide to press the "suspend access" button in the JPAS system. When that happens, the individual loses clearance until the incident is resolved. Once the incident enters the JPAS system, it is sent to the clearance adjudication facility of record. When the security officer suspends a clearance, it is then passed to clearance adjudicators to decide for or against permanently revoking the clearance. If they decide against revoking a clearance, they remove the incident report from JPAS and clearance is maintained.[50]

After receiving an incident report, a Central Adjudication Facility (CAF) may decide to request further information, such as requiring a new SF-86 in addition to a full or limited investigation of the issues raised in the incident report. Once the new investigation is complete, the CAF determines whether to leave an individual's security clearance intact or to take steps to revoke access to classified information.

As I have noted, the Obama administration supported more incident reporting; its "insider threat" policies encouraged coworkers to note and report personality traits and behaviors in colleagues that could signal an insider threat. If adjudicators determine that an investigation into the incident report is necessary, many of the conditions that could mitigate security concerns in the Adjudicative Guidelines for Determining Eligibility for Access to Classified Information are examined. In addition, after an investigation has been completed, according to the Defense Security Service, "a person trained in the process of reviewing and evaluating security clearance information reviews the results of the investigation and compares it to established qualifying criteria for eligibility to access classified national security information. Adjudicators consider the whole person, i.e., both favorable and unfavorable information, in making the clearance decision."[51]

Incident reports can make the difference between obtaining and maintaining and being denied a security clearance or having one suspended or revoked. Most incidents associated with clearance holders are reported by others. But self-reporting is also encouraged. An employee handbook reminds employees of the Department of Agriculture to self-report. According to the *Department of Agriculture Security Guide for Employees*, "All holders of a security clearance must keep their security office informed about anything that might have a bearing on their continued eligibility for access to classified information or that might signal an increased vulnerability to foreign intelligence targeting. Your cooperation in doing so is an important part of the 'continuing evaluation' process."[52] The kinds of information that must be reported by all cleared personnel are:

> Change in Personal Status: Changes in marital status, cohabitation, etc.; Foreign Travel: Whether traveling on business or pleasure; Foreign Contacts: All cleared personnel must report contacts with individuals of any foreign nationality, either within or outside the scope of their official activities; Financial Problems: This

includes filing for bankruptcy, garnishment of wages, having a lien placed upon property; Arrests: If arrested for any reason, it must be reported regardless of whether or not there was a conviction or charges were dropped for lack of evidence; Other Involvement With the Legal System: Any other involvement in legal or court proceedings; Psychological or Substance Abuse Counseling; Outside Activities: Any planned or actual outside employment or volunteer activities; Media Contacts: Any media inquiries about the job or organization should be reported; Pre-Publication Review: Any technical paper, book, magazine article, or newspaper article prepared for publication or for posting on the Internet, or lecture or speech, must be cleared in advance; Loss or Compromise of Information: If an employee inadvertently or accidentally loses or compromises classified or other sensitive information, it must be reported.[53]

Determining Eligibility for Access to Classified Information

In order to help adjudicators determine if an individual's "personal and professional history affirmatively indicates loyalty to the United States," in 2005 the White House issued Executive Order 12968, Revised Adjudicative Guidelines for Determining Eligibility for Access to Classified Information. The guidelines are used for all U.S. government civilian and military personnel, consultants, contractors, and grantees and their employees, as well as other individuals who require access to classified information. "They apply to persons being considered for initial or continued eligibility for access to classified information, to include sensitive compartmented information and special access programs, and are to be used by government departments and agencies in all final clearance determinations."

The guidelines attempt to provide a roadmap for adjudicators to vet potential and current national security workers to determine their reliability to protect classified information. The intent is to screen out individuals who are not trustworthy and to monitor those already employed in order to identify any who have become untrustworthy since their initial screening and rehabilitate or remove them. According to the guidelines, "No coercive policing could replace the self-discipline and integrity of the person entrusted with the nation's secrets as the most effective means of protecting them."[54]

When deciding whether an individual will be granted a clearance, the 2005 Revised Adjudicative Guidelines for Determining Eligibility for Access to Classified Information must be used. Any one of the thirteen guidelines may be used to grant, deny, suspend, or revoke a clearance. Below I summarize each one and then identify some of the controversies surrounding them. (The following list summarizes the Executive Order 12968, Revised Adjudicative Guidelines for Determining Eligibility for Access to Classified Information. See full text of the original executive order in the appendix).

Guideline A: Allegiance to the United States

According to the guidelines, the concern is that "an individual must be of unquestioned allegiance to the United States. The willingness to safeguard classified information is in doubt if there is any reason to suspect an individual's allegiance to the United States."

Guideline B: Foreign Influence

According to the guidelines, the concern is that "foreign contacts and interests may be a security concern if the individual has divided loyalties or foreign financial interests, may be manipulated or induced to help a foreign person, group, organization, or government in a way that is not in U.S. interests, or is vulnerable to pressure or coercion by any foreign interest."

Guideline C: Foreign Preference

According to the guidelines, the concern is that when an individual acts in such a way as to indicate a preference for a foreign country over the United States, then he or she may be prone to provide information or make decisions that are harmful to the interests of the United States.

Guideline D: Sexual Behavior

According to the guidelines, the concern is that "sexual behavior that involves a criminal offense, indicates a personality or emotional disorder, reflects lack of judgment or discretion, or which may subject the individual to undue influence or coercion, exploitation, or duress can raise questions about an individual's reliability, trustworthiness and ability to protect classified information. No adverse inference concerning the standards in the Guideline may be raised solely on the basis of the sexual orientation of the individual."

Guideline E: Personal Conduct

According to the guidelines, the concern is that "conduct involving questionable judgment, lack of candor, dishonesty, or unwillingness to comply with rules and regulations can raise questions about an individual's reliability, trustworthiness and ability to protect classified information. Of special interest is any failure to provide truthful and candid answers during the security clearance process or any other failure to cooperate with the security clearance process."

Guideline F: Financial Considerations

According to the guidelines, the concern is that "failure or inability to live within one's means, satisfy debts, and meet financial obligations may indicate poor self-control, lack of judgment, or unwillingness to abide by rules and regulations, all of which can raise questions about an individual's reliability, trustworthiness and ability to protect classified information."

Guideline G: Alcohol Consumption

According to the guidelines, the concern is that "excessive alcohol consumption often leads to the exercise of questionable judgment" or the "failure to control impulses," and can raise questions about an individual's reliability and trustworthiness.

Guideline H: Drug Involvement

According to the guidelines, the concern is that "use of an illegal drug or misuse of a prescription drug can raise questions about an individual's reliability and trustworthiness, both because it may impair judgment and because it raises questions about a person's ability or willingness to comply with laws, rules, and regulations."

Guideline I: Psychological Conditions

According to the guidelines, the concern is that "certain emotional, mental, and personality conditions can impair judgment, reliability, or trustworthiness. A formal diagnosis of a disorder is not required for concern under this guideline."

Guideline J: Criminal Conduct

According to the guidelines, the concern is that "criminal activity creates doubt about a person's judgment, reliability and trustworthiness. By its very nature, it calls into question a person's ability or willingness to comply with laws, rules and regulations."

Guideline K: Handling Protected Information

According to the guidelines, the concern is that "deliberate or negligent failure to comply with rules and regulations for protecting classified or other sensitive information raises doubt about an individual's trustworthiness, judgment, reliability, or willingness and ability to safeguard such information, and is a serious security concern."

Guideline L: Outside Activities

According to the guidelines, the concern is that "involvement in certain types of outside employment or activities is of security concern if it poses a conflict of interest with an individual's security responsibilities and could create an increased risk of unauthorized disclosure of classified information."

Guideline M: Use of Information Technology Systems

According to the guidelines, the concern is that "noncompliance with rules, procedures, guidelines or regulations pertaining to information technology systems may raise security concerns about an individual's reliability and trustworthiness, calling into question the willingness or ability to properly protect sensitive systems, networks, and information.[55]

Complications Created by the Guidelines

As the guidelines mandate, the ultimate determination of whether the security clearance is granted or maintained must be an overall common-sense judgment based on careful consideration of the individual guidelines, "each of which is to be evaluated in the context of the whole person." But news reports have revealed instances in which some guidelines have proven problematic.

COMPLICATIONS ASSOCIATED WITH GUIDELINE F:
FINANCIAL CONSIDERATIONS

The mitigating factors associated with an employee's or potential employee's financial circumstances include determining if "the conditions that resulted in the financial problem were largely beyond the person's control (e.g. loss of employment, a business downturn, unexpected medical emergency, or a death, divorce or separation)," but they do not take into account incidents wherein the government itself has forced an individual into a financial crisis. As the *Baltimore Sun* reported, military service members must change duty stations when ordered. In an unfavorable real estate market, a move can place them in the position of having to sell a home at a loss. The government does not routinely take this circumstance into consideration when making clearance determinations:

> Air Force Maj. Justice Sakyi's change-of-station orders to Germany came with a built-in dilemma: what to do about his family's home in Maryland. He and his wife, Olivia, bought the single-family house in Bowie in early 2006, near the height of the housing bubble. Then came the bust. Selling for what they owe is impossible. They can't rent the place out for nearly enough to cover the mortgage. And they haven't been able to negotiate a lower payment. About 185,000 service members who own homes get orders to relocate each year, according to the Consumer Financial Protection Bureau. . . . "If circumstances are outside of a service member's control—in other words, they own a home and they're being required to [make a] permanent change

of station . . . a short sale may be the most responsible step they can take and they will not be looked at unfavorably," said Maj. Shawn McKelvy, deputy director of legal policy for the Office of the Under Secretary of Defense for Personnel and Readiness.[56]

While the guidelines do not single out congressional ineptitude as a mitigating factor in an individual's financial concerns, some lawmakers voiced concern about the plight of security clearance holders caught in the last round of sequestration. *Government Executive* magazine reports on the concerns of Senator Susan Collins, who represents the clearance holders at the Portsmouth Naval Shipyard in Maine:

> A top Republican senator is concerned that furloughs resulting from the sequester could endanger some federal employees' security clearances. Susan Collins of Maine has asked the agency that handles the government security clearance process not to rescind employees' credentials because of financial problems stemming solely from being furloughed. "I understand the reason a security clearance could be revoked for an employee who is in financial trouble because of decisions he or she made," Collins wrote. . . . "In these unusual circumstances, however, employees may have financial difficulties due to the unexpected impact of sequestration." The government can revoke the security clearances of federal employees who fall into financial debt, which in turn can cost them their jobs since some positions require those credentials. Many agencies have said they will have to furlough. . . . As a result, some federal employees will have trouble keeping up with expenses and could miss monthly car or mortgage payments, for example.[57]

COMPLICATIONS ASSOCIATED WITH GUIDELINE H:
DRUG INVOLVEMENT

This guideline has as a mitigating factor "satisfactory completion of a prescribed drug treatment program," but Pauline Jelinek, writing for *the Huffington Post*, reports on a study by the National Academies of Sciences, Engineering, and Medicine (the Academies) Health and Medicine Division (HMD) formerly Institute of Medicine (IOM).

The study says military members often do not get the help they need to overcome alcohol and drug addiction:

"Better care for service members and their families is hampered by inadequate prevention strategies, staffing shortages, . . . and stigma associated with these disorders," said Charles P. O'Brien of the University of Pennsylvania's Center for Studies of Addiction. . . . "We reviewed the training materials the U.S. Navy uses for counselor training. Those materials are based on guidelines originally written in 1984. They haven't updated them." . . . Today, the military's approach to treating substance abuse "tends to be old-fashioned," O'Brien said, noting the example of the military's reluctance to use medications that can combat cravings and in other ways help treat addiction. . . . "Modern treatment of substance abuse does involve medications. There are FDA-approved, effective medications that could be used and should be used much more than they are," he said.[58]

COMPLICATIONS ASSOCIATED WITH GUIDELINE I:
PSYCHOLOGICAL CONDITIONS

In 2009 the Defense Centers of Excellence for Psychological Health and Traumatic Brain Injury launched the "Real Warriors Campaign" to help military personnel overcome the stigma associated with seeking psychological help. The aim of the program is to encourage military personnel to seek help when they need it. The campaign uses social networking, radio, television, posters, flyers, and a website featuring stories of real service members who have sought treatment and are continuing to serve. The implication is that if you seek mental health treatment you will not lose your clearance. But Surgeon General of the Army Eric Schoomaker did not say that during an interview about the campaign. Schoomaker emphasized lowering the stigma, but said nothing about keeping clearance: "One of our challenges is to lower the stigma of [soldiers] getting follow-on counseling. . . . Human beings exposed to trauma in life have fairly high frequency of developing symptoms later on. It's a normal human reaction."[59]

Robert Guzzo's parents say the Navy cautioned him not to seek mental health treatment for symptoms of post-traumatic stress disorder before he committed suicide on Veterans Day 2012. Guzzo's father told *Washington Post TV* that his son was worried about losing his security clearance.[60] " 'They told him specifically not to report on any worksheet that you are having these issues, because if they do, they'll take your bird. They'll take your trident,' [Guzzo's father] told the *Post*. The Navy denies that service members who seek treatment for Post-Traumatic Stress Disorder (PTSD) face negative career consequences. 'I'm not going to hide how he died,' Andersen told the *Post*. 'People need to know this is what happened and it could happen to other veterans.' "[61] But as Gillum and Tucker reported for the Associated Press, Chairman of the Joint Chiefs of Staff Martin Dempsey still believes that those who have served in the military should not have to answer questions about mental health treatment or status on security clearance forms:

> In recent years, Dempsey and other military leaders had argued that service members—many of whom have been plagued by stress disorders and other problems after multiple deployments in more than a decade of war—should have the opportunity to overcome their mental health challenges without being stigmatized. He questioned whether forcing Alexis to disclose that he had been undergoing mental health treatments could have prevented . . . tragedy. "I don't know what the investigation will determine, but he committed murder," said Dempsey . . . "and I'm not sure that any particular question or lack of question on a security clearance form would probably have revealed that."[62]

Dempsey's doubts demonstrate the complexity of this task. Alexis's propensity for murder would not be reflected in his application forms because he had not demonstrated it yet. That is a large part of the problem. It is very difficult to predict and monitor future human behavior on the basis of current information. Even if such unchecked behavior (or potential behavior) exists in an applicant's past, it is highly unlikely to rise to the surface during a background investigation. As John Sullivan notes, after thirty-one years conducting polygraph exams for the CIA, "The only admission of murder I ever obtained from an applicant occurred during a pretest. In response to the question about having committed a serious crime, the subject said, 'Well yeah, I killed somebody once.' When I asked for details, the man said that he had stabbed a man in a fight and was pretty sure he had killed him."[63]

Whatever the Pentagon's report on the Navy Yard shooting reveals about that individual's psychological treatment and the reporting of it, the complexities surrounding the disclosure of mental health treatment of security clearance applicants and what that may mean for national security will remain controversial.

COMPLICATIONS ASSOCIATED WITH GUIDELINE J: CRIMINAL CONDUCT

This issue is also coming to light in the case of Navy contractor Aaron Alexis's shooting rampage at the Washington Navy Yard. Alexis was granted a security clearance and credentials to enter the facility even though investigators had determined that he had a criminal record. An article in *The Guardian* reported that Alexis was granted a secret security clearance even after an FBI database search revealed he had apparently lied about an arrest on his application form: "An internal inquiry has established that when Alexis first enlisted, in June 2007, he declared on a security questionnaire that he had never been arrested. However, a fingerprint check on an FBI database revealed that he had been arrested three years previously. . . . He was still granted a special security clearance, after attending an interview and claiming that he did not think he needed to declare the arrest."[64]

COMPLICATIONS ASSOCIATED WITH GUIDELINE K: HANDLING PROTECTED INFORMATION

Thomas Drake, a former employee at the U.S. National Security Agency (NSA), after going through internal channels unsuccessfully, contacted Siobhan Gorman, a journalist at the *Baltimore Sun*. According to Drake, he was careful not to disclose classified information to her, but he did provide her with enough information to successfully report on the government waste, fraud, and abuse that he had witnessed at the NSA.[65] But the administration's lawyers alleged that Drake "mishandled" documents and threatened to send him to prison under the Espionage Act of 1917. At his trial, the judge ruled that "there is no evidence that Reporter A relied upon any allegedly classified information found in Mr. Drake's house in her articles."[66] Eventually, all ten original espionage charges against Drake were dropped. He pled guilty to one misdemeanor count for exceeding authorized use of a computer. In Drake's case, there is no question that he embarrassed the NSA, and thereby the administration. But would that call into question his ability to keep legitimate national security secrets? The *Washington Post* editorial board was concerned that the administration might have been too punitive and that its actions could have a chilling effect on future whistleblowers:

> Mr. Drake, a former employee of the National Security Agency, did not hand information to al-Qaeda. His alleged crime: communicating with a *Baltimore Sun* reporter about an NSA surveillance program that he believed had been grossly mismanaged and was wasting billions of taxpayer dollars. . . . The question here is whether the indictment and proposed punishment are proportionate to the alleged infraction. . . . At times, revocation of security clearances may be the most appropriate action; dismissal and prosecution may be called for when more serious violations are confirmed. Mr. Drake's prosecution smacks of overkill and could scare others with legitimate concerns about government programs from coming forward.[67]

Note that the *Washington Post* editorial board differentiated between the two punishments—losing one's clearance and losing one's job—displaying the naïve supposition that they do not have one and the same result for an employee in Drake's position.

COMPLICATIONS ASSOCIATED WITH GUIDELINE L: OUTSIDE ACTIVITIES

Dr. Abdel-Moniem ibn Ali El-Ganayni is an Egyptian-born American nuclear physicist who formerly worked for the Department of

Energy's (DOE) Bettis Atomic Power Laboratory in Philadelphia. His work at the lab required a clearance. In October 2007 his clearance was suspended, effectively barring him from any work at Bettis. He asked to appeal the suspension; however, El-Ganayni's right to appeal was denied, and the DOE would not tell him why it had suspended his clearance. But before his suspension he had been interviewed by DOE security officials, and later the FBI. In those interviews he was questioned about his political beliefs, his religious views, and his work as an imam in the Philadelphia prison system. No questions related to his work or any potential breaches of security were asked in either interview.[68] The interviews focused on El-Ganayni's criticism of American foreign policy and the FBI's mistreatment of Muslims after September 11, 2001. Specifically, El-Ganayni expressed concern about an FBI raid of a Pittsburgh mosque during Friday prayers, where attendees were searched and forced to stand outside while being questioned. After his clearance was revoked, the American Civil Liberties Union (ACLU) filed a lawsuit on his behalf alleging that the DOE revoked his clearance because he had criticized the FBI and U.S. foreign policy. The suit demanded that the DOE reveal the allegations against El-Ganayni and restore due process, allowing him to contest any allegations made against him.[69]

Sally Kalson, reporting for the *Pittsburgh Post-Gazette*, noted that the FBI's claim that national security had been jeopardized was "invoked solely to shield the agency from having to disclose the unconstitutional retaliatory and discriminatory reasons for its action. In reality, [the ACLU] says, the decision was made 'because he is a foreign-born Muslim who has spoken publicly and critically about U.S. foreign policy and the FBI's treatment of Muslims.'" Further, "'Many [native-born] Americans say what I say about the war,' Dr. El-Ganayni said yesterday. 'But when I say it, I become a traitor. I want to show that the laws apply to me the same as to any other citizen.'"[70]

In another incident reported by the *Washington Post,* Mahmoud M. Hegab, a former budget analyst for the National Geospatial-Intelligence Agency (NGA), told officials during his orientation that he had gotten married between the time of his security clearance investigation and the date he reported to work. The agency revoked his clearance, citing concerns about his wife's background as a program associate with Islamic Relief USA, a global nonprofit. The organization provides food aid and public health and education programs in poor and disaster-prone regions. According to the *Washington Post*:

> Hegab's attorney argued in court papers that the decision to revoke his client's clearance "was based solely" on his wife's religion, Islam, "her constitutionally protected speech, and her association with, and employment by, an Islamic faith-based organization." . . . During the course of its investigation, the NGA discovered a photo believed to be of [Hegab's wife] attending a 2003 anti-Iraq war protest in Washington—when she was 16 years old. . . . Hegab said his wife attended the anti-war rally along with thousands of other Americans, including military veterans and lawmakers. . . . The NGA told Hegab that he lost his clearance because of . . . [his wife's] "current affiliation with one or more organizations which consist of groups who are organized largely around their non-United States origin."[71]

COMPLICATIONS ASSOCIATED WITH GUIDELINE M:
USE OF INFORMATION TECHNOLOGY SYSTEMS

Edward Snowden, the former NSA employee who leaked classified agency documents to members of the press, identified himself as a whistleblower and alleged the NSA was running unconstitutional programs and lying to Congress and the American people about it. But as CBS News reported at the time, the NSA left the door open for someone like Snowden to obtain and release documents by using antiquated IT security methods. Security experts also admit that part of the problem with "insider threats" like Snowden may be that so many people have clearance:

> When Edward Snowden stole the crown jewels of the National Security Agency, he didn't need to use any sophisticated devices or software or go around any computer firewall. All he needed,

said multiple intelligence community sources, was a few thumb drives and the willingness to exploit a gaping hole in an antiquated security system to rummage at will through the NSA's servers and take 20,000 documents without leaving a trace. . . . "U.S. intelligence has invited so many people into the secret realm," said an intelligence official. "There are potentially tons of Edward Snowdens. But most people aren't willing to vacuum everything up and break the law."[72]

According to the administration and defense officials, Snowden is a traitor for breaking his oath to keep classified documents secret, thereby putting national security at risk. But Snowden maintains that the government is at fault. "I swore an oath to defend the Constitution of the United States and I witnessed NSA violating it on a massive scale. I knew what I had to do. I kept my oath."[73]

This review of the mechanisms used to process individuals through the clearance system has shown how the system sometimes fails those within it. News reports focus on some of the obvious failures: investigators are at times overworked, negligent, or dishonest; databases designed to "connect the dots" can be incomplete and unreliable; methodologies for accurately assessing and identifying behavioral and personality disorders are nascent; the scientific basis for the polygraph is questionable; and random drug tests can be inaccurate.

Without denying the need for some sort of bureaucracy of secrecy, I have mapped out some of the complications that ensue when the bureaucracy designed to protect its secrets fails. As I hope is obvious, the process is not as rigorously scientific as many would hope (or assume) it to be. Next I explore how individuals, when challenged by the system, experience it firsthand.

1. Julius and Ethel Rosenberg were convicted of espionage for passing atomic secrets to the Soviet Union. They were executed in the electric chair at Sing Sing Correctional Facility in New York State on June 19, 1953. Courtesy of the National Archives (Photo Number 65-CC-52-5).

2. J. Robert Oppenheimer, the nation's most famous nuclear scientist who headed the Manhattan Project, a secret weapons program. In 1953, Oppenheimer was told that his security clearance had been suspended. After a subsequent hearing, Americans learned that the Atomic Energy Commission had revoked the security clearance for the "Father of the Atomic Bomb." Courtesy of the National Archives (Photo Number 434-OR-7-45).

3. Robert Philip Hanssen, a former FBI agent who spied for Soviet Union and Russian intelligence services against the United States for twenty-two years. He sold secrets for more than $1.4 million in cash and diamonds. According to the U.S. Department of Justice's Commission for the Review of FBI Security Programs he is "possibly the worst intelligence disaster in U.S. history." Currently serving fifteen consecutive life sentences. © Reuters Pictures.

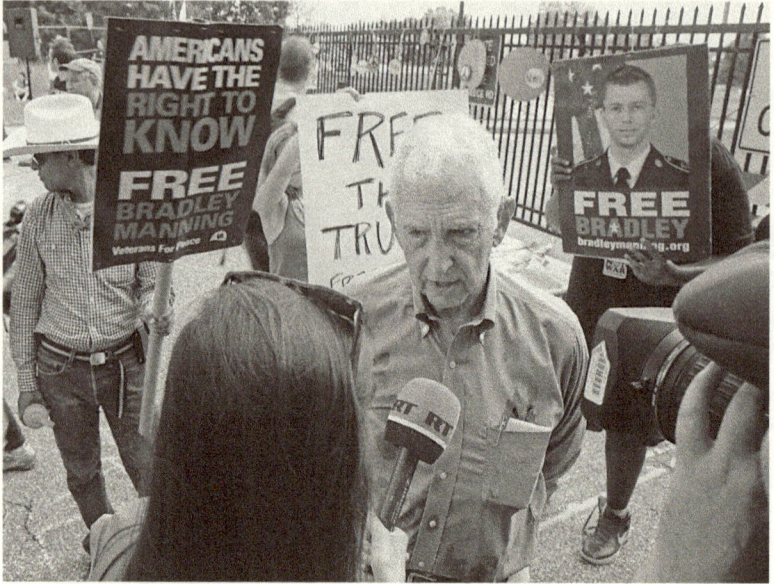

4. Daniel Ellsberg leaked the Pentagon Papers in 1971 to the *New York Times* and other newspapers. He was charged under the Espionage Act of 1917 along with other charges of theft and conspiracy, carrying a total maximum sentence of 115 years. Due to governmental misconduct and illegal evidence gathering, all charges against him were dismissed in May of 1973. Shown at protest to free Chelsea—earlier known as Bradley—Manning. © Jonathan Ernst/Reuters Pictures.

5. Edward Snowden, an American computer specialist and National Security Agency (NSA) contractor, worked for the CIA and NSA before leaking details of several top-secret United States and British government mass surveillance programs to the press. The retaliation against Snowden was immediate. © Andre Kelly/Reuters Pictures.

6. Walter Kendall Myers is a retired U.S. State Department officer who, with his wife, Gwendolyn, was arrested and indicted in June of 2009 on charges of spying for Cuba for nearly thirty years. On July 16, 2010, Kendall was sentenced to life imprisonment without possibility of parole. Gwendolyn was sentenced to a total of eighty-one months in prison. According to law enforcement officials, "The couple were 'true believers' in the Cuban system." © Ho New/Reuters Pictures.

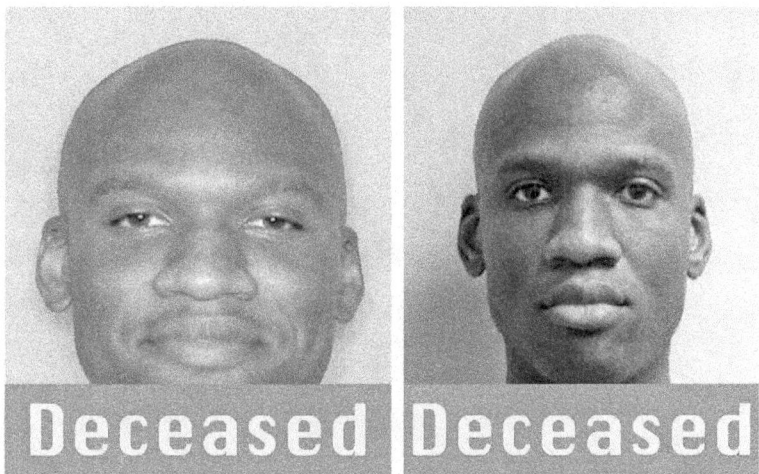

Deceased Deceased

7. Navy reservist Aaron Alexis killed twelve people in a 2013 shooting rampage inside the Washington DC Navy Yard. Incensed, Congress called for then-Secretary of Defense Chuck Hagel to reform the clearance system to prevent individuals with personality disorders from obtaining clearance. © Reuters Pictures.

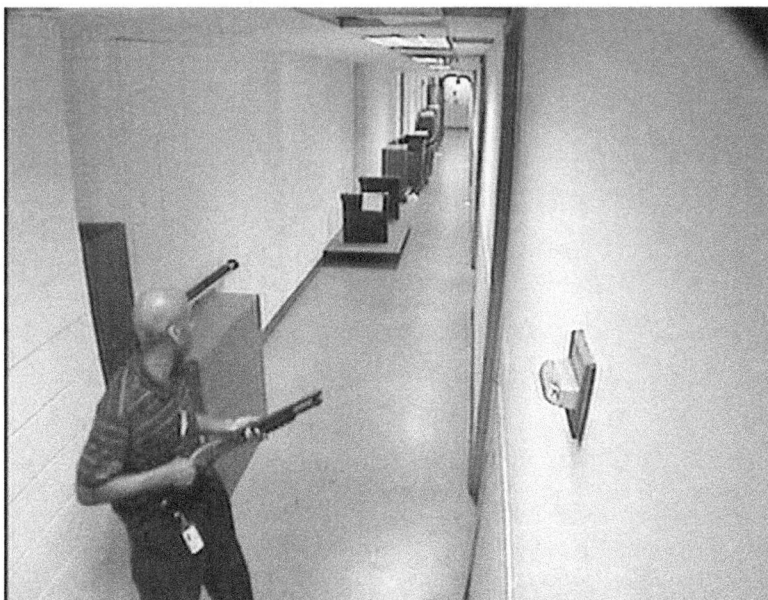

8. Security camera photos captured Alexis walking the halls of the NAVSEA Building 197, wielding his Remington 870 Express Tactical 12-gauge shotgun. © Reuters Pictures.

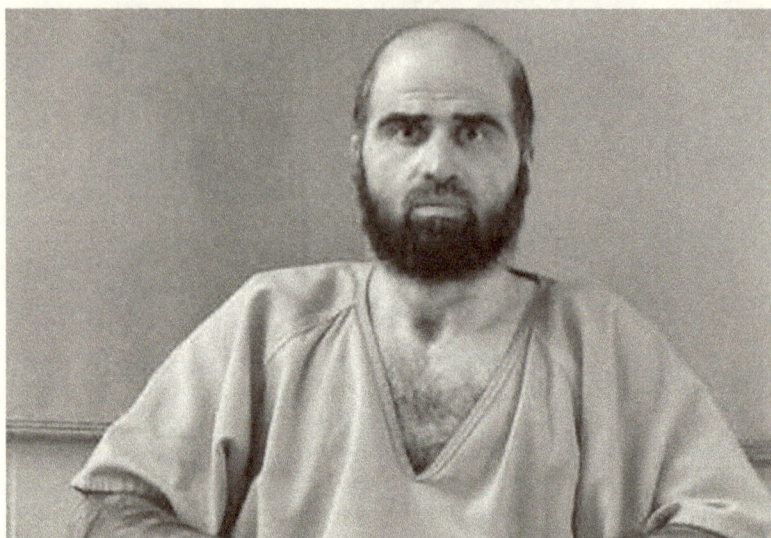

9. Nidal Malik Hasan, a U.S. Army major and psychiatrist who killed thirteen people and injured more than thirty at Fort Hood, Texas, in 2009, demonstrates the difficulty of closing gaps in the personnel security clearance process surrounding mental health issues and granting and maintaining security clearances. © Reuters Pictures.

10. Chelsea Elizabeth Manning, a United States Army intelligence analyst, was convicted in July 2013 of violations of the Espionage Act and other offenses after releasing U.S. diplomatic and Army cables to WikiLeaks, and was sentenced to thirty-five years in prison. © Gary Cameron/Reuters Pictures.

11. Chelsea Manning. During the trial, media attention quickly focused on Manning's intent to undergo hormone therapy, with news outlets airing a photo, released by the Pentagon, of Manning wearing a wig and lipstick. © Reuters Pictures.

3   Running Afoul of the System

"I believe what you say," said the flogger, "but . . . I've been
hired to flog and flog I will."
—Franz Kafka, *The Trial*

In this chapter you will learn what people told me about their experiences with the national personnel security clearance system. I started
the interviews with lawyers who represent government workers
who have lost clearances. I then spoke with clients of those lawyers
about their experiences. I also spoke with government security professionals who work within the system, Capitol Hill staffers, and
run-of-the-mill government workers, some of whom were my friends
and colleagues. I interviewed these people over a two-year period.

While I am aware of the methodological limitations of my process, I believe that what these people have articulated illuminates
the complex and sometimes problematic power relationship between
individual government workers and the state that they have sworn to
serve. I nearly always came away from these discussions with three
distinct yet related feelings: sympathy for the individuals caught in
the overwhelming power imbalance between the individual and the
state (including both those who maintain power structures and those
who run afoul of them); respect for the enthusiasm and energy with
which individuals serve the nation and express their love of country;
and admiration for the resilience with which those who have lost

a clearance recover from that loss and the strength of those who continue to maintain and work within the system.

In my discussions, I found nearly unanimous support for a clearance system, along with an understanding that the current system is flawed. Many believe that the emphasis on individual components of the system (such as security interviews, investigations, polygraph exams) is misplaced, clearing spies (like Aldridge Ames) and leakers (like Edward Snowden) for access to classified information while severing other, more loyal, employees from productive service. They see the system as overflowing with what statistical researchers call type I and type II errors; a type I error is detecting an effect that is not present (a false positive), while a type II error is failing to detect an effect that is present (resulting in a false negative).

My interviewees, who included individuals and their family members, described how losing a clearance made them feel about their own identity, often citing feelings of isolation and depression. Families are important support structures for individuals, but they can also crumble under the full weight of bureaucratic animus.

Patriotism is one trait that all of those I interviewed share. So it is no surprise that many were astonished to find themselves—after choosing careers in service to their country's ideals, such as constitutional rights and due process—denied basic rights when confronted by the state they served. Most federal workers never lose a security clearance, so these individual experiences are not the standard. For this reason they are uniquely descriptive of the complex power relationship between individuals and the state. Out of respect for their privacy, I used pseudonyms for all of the interviewees.

Unanimous Agreement on the Need for Clearance

All interviewees had a strong understanding of the importance of national security to the state they have been cleared to protect, and it is notable that nearly all of them believed that some kind of clearance process is necessary. All interviewees were resigned to participating in that process.

Daniel, an attorney who represents clients who have had security clearance revoked, makes the point that even those who have run afoul of the system tend to seek leniency within it, rarely a way around it. "Having dealt with many people who've lost their clearance or had their clearance under scrutiny, I don't think I've ever heard anybody actually criticize the need for the process or say, 'The system shouldn't care about that.' Now, they may complain about the individual circumstance, like, 'They're being too strict with the rule. They're not being fair to me.' But there seems to be pretty universal understanding that we need the system."

Martin, another attorney who represents those who challenge personnel actions related to security clearance, also articulates the normative response regarding the personnel security clearance system. "Well, let me say this. If I did something where I deserved to lose my clearance and they caught me and I lost my clearance, I don't think I would have anything to complain about. I wouldn't feel the system was unjust."

In the early 2000s Doug began a legal career after retiring from the U.S. Marine Corps, where he served with Special Forces units in Afghanistan and Iraq. He describes the normative national security discourse surrounding the need for clearance. "The common-sense answer is there's no way to avoid responsibly having a system to do our best that the folks that review classified information are trustworthy. It's information that could endanger the lives of our intelligence operatives, reveal our sources and methods of secret national security missions. It's as old as the concept of spying that we don't want the enemy to be privy to that material in advance. . . . To me it's a no-brainer."

Individuals who have lost a clearance—either through their own actions or as victims of the system's failures—also see the process as inevitable and important in determining individual commitment and loyalty to the nation. Some also cite other perceived benefits of the system that include screening for individual suitability and filtering out individuals with potentially negative characteristics or personality traits.

Frederick lost his security clearance at the Department of Defense in what was later determined, by the secretary of defense, among others, to be a whistleblowing incident:

I think it's very important in the sense that you want people who support the constitutional foundations of this country to be hired in a way that . . . guarantees that they're gonna be supporting that. You don't wanna hire people that would potentially work against the best interest of the state. . . . You can weed out crazies. You can weed out people who are easily incentivized by bad things. Corrupt. You can weed out personality types. . . . I don't know how else to put it. I think it's essential if you wanna have a functional government that survives over time—a functional Department of Defense, for example—you've gotta know something about the people you're hiring, and you've gotta have a choice on that. You want people who will promote the mission and not work against it.

Jill is a supervisor at an intelligence agency. Part of her job is to cooperate with security investigators conducting initial and reinvestigations of personnel under her supervision. She sees this responsibility as an important part of her work. "You have to know who it is you're trusting with all these security issues, sensitive information. We have a responsibility to the people who are already serving in government to make sure that their coworkers are trustworthy. It has to all be a trustworthy team. And we're obliged to do that."

Flaws in the System

The sense that the system provides a useful mechanism for weeding out inappropriate hires is pervasive and is seen as necessary. But many also acknowledge that the system is flawed. Individuals suggest reasons for the system's flaws ranging from an inefficient use of technology to a bloated bureaucracy, limited budgets and other resources, and the imperfect science of predicting human behavior. Those who study and criticize the system, and those who participate in and perpetuate it, say that little is being done to improve the system and to fight consequent abuses.

Stanley runs an institute for the study of government and military power. While he is aware of the flaws in the system, he also acknowledges the difficulties posed by the complexities of designing a system that works for such a large number of people:

> I think the security clearance system can be understood as an effort to accomplish the nearly impossible task of ensuring the trustworthiness of the workforce. I say it's an effort and it's nearly impossible because we know it sometimes fails. People with the highest clearances occasionally go astray, engage in espionage on behalf of a foreign power or in other kinds of illegal activity. But it's a consequence of the bureaucratization of the national security apparatus. There are millions of people in the system. There is no way for any one person or group of people to be assured of the trustworthiness or patriotism of all of the other members without some sort of procedural filter. And so the security clearance system, as it has developed, is the best that anyone has come up with up to now. It is flawed. It involves both false positives and false negatives. That is, people get through the system who are not trustworthy. People get excluded from the system who are perfectly patriotic and trustworthy. So like any bureaucratic institution, it is defective. And yet it seems to fill a requirement.

Many respondents note that, as large as the clearance task is, its requirements are constantly growing. Charles is a psychiatrist who has a security clearance and counsels individuals with security clearances. "The whole system . . . is maybe intrinsically almost impossible to pull off that well anyhow. With post-9/11, there's been such a huge growth in everything connected with security that I think it's literally exponential the amount of clearances that were called for, which I think just stressed the system to the max."

Many respondents also expressed concerns that, while the system is flawed, they must work within it, often hoping for the best while bracing for the worst. Throughout the interview process, I detected a level of stress in some respondents—part of which I attributed to talking to me and part to the polymorphous dangers associated with national security work. Megan, who works on Capitol Hill as a staffer on a congressional committee, hits on an underlying and recurring theme in the efficacy of the system: its dubious reliability.

"It's analogous to when the lone gunman walked into the Capitol and shot those two police officers and was trying to shoot other people. If there's a lone person who's basically bound and determined to release classified information, they're gonna release classified information, and it won't matter how many background investigations you've done of them."

As Megan notes, background investigations are conducted as part of the personnel clearance process. To better understand this aspect of the process, let us explore some of the flaws within the personnel security clearance vetting process.

Problems with Background Investigations and Interviews

According to Executive Order 12968 signed by President Clinton in 1995, an "appropriate investigation" must be completed to determine if an applicant's "personal and professional history affirmatively indicates loyalty to the United States." Prospective job seekers must submit consent forms before an investigation process can begin. Those forms authorize the release of any and all background information to security clearance investigators. Also during the investigation, investigators try to uncover any involvement with drugs, encounters with the police, drinking habits, and other facts about personal history. Investigators try to obtain both favorable and unfavorable information about an applicant so that adjudicators can make an appropriate clearance determination.[1]

This process has come under scrutiny in the wake of publicized clearance infractions. In some cases, private companies were found negligent. For example, in 2012 a number of former employees of U.S. Investigations Services Inc. (USIS), the largest private contractor handling background checks for the government, were charged with falsifying records.[2] I discuss that incident further later in this chapter.

Even when interviews are conducted by government employees in accordance with standardized methods and regulations, they sometimes come up short. Hugh Gusterson, a professor at George Mason University, notes that students often list him as a reference. He is amused by, as he calls it, the "formulaic idiocy" of the questions investigators ask. For example, when investigators ask about drug use, he can only reply, "They certainly haven't done any drugs around me."

One of the problems with investigations is that the same faulty methods used to screen potential candidates are also used to revoke the clearances of existing employees. As a supervisor in a federal agency, Jill must cooperate with security investigations and reinvestigations of personnel under her supervision. Although she has participated in hundreds of security investigations and interviews over the years, and sees the responsibility to do so as an important part of her job, she also has doubts about the efficacy of the interviews. She does not recommend specific changes, but feels the current process is merely scratching the surface:

> Well, having been a federal employee for zillions of years, I know what the process is, and also being a supervisor I know. I don't even like it when the interviewers come in and interview about a person. It is such a checklist. . . . It's a rote thing. It's not about the real person. You are given an opportunity to say something about a person, but the questions are so routine and so rote, and I really don't think they really explore who the person is. And I'm not sure, like I can't really conceive of a better way of doing that, to be honest with you. You know, ask your coworkers, ask your friends, but. . . . It's okay for the initial screening, definitely. You're going to get a sense of a person, whether they're trustworthy and all that. You're going to get a sense. But if there's a question, I don't think that's adequate.

Charles is a psychiatrist who holds a security clearance and counsels patients who hold security clearances. He also participates frequently in interviews conducted by investigators. Charles too questions the usefulness of the interviews. He too fails to recommend changes but voices concern that investigators depend on him to identify impediments to the candidate's clearance:

> I think there are real limitations to it, because it is just a filter, and I know, because I get visited all the time by officers of one agency

or the other for people that I see as patients. At the present time, I can get by with just simply answering one question with the answer "no" and that's the whole deal. . . . It's very thin support for anything that's of any depth to have such a limitation. It's a one-pager, and there's a block at the bottom, that's the key one that you can literally check off a box that says yes or no, and the question is precisely—I don't remember the exact wording of it—but "Do you have any reason to be concerned about" blah, blah, blah? All I have to do is say "no" and that's the end of the story in nearly all cases. Now, it's true they do follow-up BIs [background investigations] five years out. I understand that. But again, I'm not terribly impressed that they're all that thorough, though how one does this in the real world, God only knows.

Andy held a clearance for twenty years at the Department of Defense before losing it in 2010 in a whistleblowing incident. He has some ideas about improving the efficacy of interviews. He believes investigators should interview a wider array of acquaintances, rather than interviewing neighbors, which is standard practice. He questions how reliable neighbors are as references in contemporary urban and suburban neighborhoods because people move frequently and often do not know their neighbors. He also expressed surprise that standard practices for investigations do not currently include analyses of candidates' social media presence:

> The . . . thing that obviously I think they don't do enough of is talk—for example, to the people I work with, or the people I both served in combat with or I've known for 30 years, some of the people on my Facebook, for example. . . . If there's things regarding my reliability, I have no problem with people looking at my Facebook. . . . [rather than] talking to your neighbors [and asking] "Hey, is he a good guy? Does he put his Christmas lights up on a timely basis and take 'em down before January 15th?" It's insane.

Andy's recommendation for monitoring social networks may be the way things are moving. The Associated Press reported, during congressional hearings on improving the security clearance process, that a new methodology for constant monitoring of workers' online activities is under development.[3]

What Are the Limits on Investigators and Interviewers?

In addition to the investigations that occur during the application process, individuals are often interviewed by investigators who must provide details for readjudication, once a clearance is in question. Such interviews can be unsettling for individuals who, in some cases, do not know what (if anything) they have done to occasion additional scrutiny. In most cases, individuals are unaware of the parameters within which investigators may navigate. My research found that, for women in particular, interviews sustain an already uncomfortable power dynamic when questions by male interviewers can skew to a sexual nature.[4]

As John Sullivan noted, during his thirty-one-year career as a polygrapher that began in 1968, at the CIA detailed sexual specifics were included in reports compiled on female subjects but not on males. Indeed there were times when the CIA apparently considered any sexual activity whatsoever on the part of female employees noteworthy. "Regarding the reporting of heterosexual activity, in all the reports that I read . . . I rarely saw a comment on the heterosexual activities of a male. A case could be made that the Office of Security was . . . sexist, with a tinge of racism thrown in. On one memorable occasion, I picked up a file for my morning case and in reading the [background investigation] saw the notation, 'subject dates blacks!' underlined. When I went to pick up this female subject, I was rather surprised to find that she was an African American."[5]

Laura, a long-time federal employee, was interviewed by agency security officers after it was reported that she had befriended a foreign national (whom she subsequently married) while on detail abroad. Because of the friendship and subsequent romance her clearance was revoked and she was summoned for a face-to-face interview at the personnel security office. She describes the incident as "traumatic" primarily because of the invasive sexual nature of the questions and her discomfort at not knowing what boundaries (if any) the interrogators were obliged to maintain. She spoke to me, through her tears, about the power dynamic between herself and the investigators:

> The agency and OPM [Office of Personnel Management] investigators . . . there's a potential for a lot of abuse of authority. There don't seem to be very many checks on the kinds of things they can ask. . . . It's really hard to identify what exactly their boundaries are, and there's really no one to ask, and you're in this very—I don't know how to explain it—I guess an analogy would be like if you're a prison guard and a prisoner. They're in a position of authority, so you don't want to push too hard, because they hold the keys. So with the people that do this, it's really hard to know what their boundaries are, and you're kind of—or at least I was—a little afraid to push on things that I thought maybe were inappropriate. Because what if they get mad, and your job is . . . on the line. So they came and they interviewed me and it was one of the most traumatic experiences of my life basically, because they were so invasive.

It was difficult for Laura to discuss the nature of the questions she was forced to answer, although she did say that agents asked her where she had had sex, and in which sexual position(s).

This proves not an uncommon experience for women who find themselves in a power struggle with the state. Reporting on the 2013 trial of three male cadets accused of raping a fellow female cadet at the Naval Academy, *Time* magazine described the "graphic, repetitive questions" the victim endured during her interrogations. "The lawyers wanted to know if she wore underwear . . . how wide she opens her mouth during oral sex and if she 'grinds' while dancing."[6]

The state's methodology seems to be behind the times (and the rest of society) when it comes to battling sexual violence. The executive agencies of the federal government like to make their own rules in meting out justice to their workers. One need only look at the repeated failed attempts (by female legislators and others) to wrest power over military rape victims' fate from the military.[7] The fact that the state is behind the times when it comes to gender bias (among other things) is apparent to some in Congress and also to many in the academy who study the issue.

Laura describes the incident as traumatic not only because of the sexual nature of the questions or the way she was treated by investigators but also because she was not told (until the interview) why she was being questioned. When she asked her supervisor what was happening, the supervisor simply said, "I'm sorry, I can't share it with you."

Problems with Self-Reporting

Security offices encourage individuals to "self-report" any relevant security incident. According to the Personnel Security Office Guidelines of the U.S. Department of Agriculture, "All holders of a security clearance must keep their security office informed about anything that might have a bearing on their continued eligibility for access to classified information or that might signal an increased vulnerability to foreign intelligence targeting."[8]

Laura notes that some of the troubles she endured might have been mitigated if she had "self-reported" her romance. She said that part of the reason she did not report the romantic encounter was that she did not see it as important at the time. But the other reason was that she feared the moral judgments of others. "So not as an excuse, but as an explanation, I didn't disclose the full nature of my relationship with [the person] who is now my husband. Honestly, I didn't really ever intend for it to go that far, and it was a one-night thing, but it was fear. It was like, they're not going to understand. They're going to think whatever."

Andy, on the other hand, always kept investigators informed of his activities. He developed a positive relationship with the personnel security team at his agency and was confident that they had his best interests in mind—until he became convinced they did not. Since his clearance was revoked, he worries that information he self-reported to investigators and security specialists will be used against him.

> During the early days of the security process . . . I had no problem being totally honest with my investigator. As a matter of

fact, I would call out of cycle and just say, "Look, this is what's going on. I'm doing X, Y and Z." I had no problem saying, "This is something I'm sure is of concern, but even though it may be of concern, it's not gonna be used against me because I'm telling you about it." Therefore, I felt, for example, if I was sleeping with someone that may be married, it's like, "Here's the deal. I'm sleeping with her. And they can't blackmail me on it because I've already told you about it." "I'm having a drinking problem and this is what I'm doing about it." I felt totally able to talk about my personal problems and be a human being. Now I see how the security clearance system has become something used to really just hammer people for personal faults. You have to be almost a warrior monk, if you will, to sustain yourself in the current system, because you can't be a human being and just say, "I've got a problem. These are the things I have to do to fix it. I'm working on it." And to me, the whole idea should be that you take and give the system the information so they can say, "It can't be used against him to blackmail him." That's the whole issue. Instead, it becomes something that is used to hammer people for their personal growth issues. Look, I'm no saint . . . I don't hide the fact that I'm no saint. With that said, I'm not a threat to national security. I do everything I can to support the country.

Given Andy's experience, Laura may have been right to fear the moral judgments associated with self-reporting. Most of us are not warrior monks. Laura also worries about the possibly unattainable standards to which cleared government workers are held. Her concern is that the pressure to be above suspicion at all times will cause undue stress to workers in the long term.

It doesn't have to be that way, because people have problems. There's just got to be some reform, so that you can actually be a normal person like everybody else and have your problems or whatever, without somebody questioning your integrity and your suitability for government employment, because you have a lousy husband, or because you had a bad break, because you're upside down on your house because of the economy. . . . But government employees are held to a higher standard. That's another thing. I was underwater in my house in [X], and I held on to it and made payments to it because I was like, "Oh my God. I don't want to lose my job." Normal people don't have to deal with these things.

Problems with the Polygraph

In chapter 2, I noted that the National Academy of Sciences found that polygraph examinations are dangerously unreliable and advised the federal government to cease depending on them to screen for security risks. And there are other critics of the polygraph as a tool to screen prospective and existing employees. In 1983 the U.S. Congress's Office of Technology Assessment (OTA), determined that the polygraph was not a scientifically valid tool for screening government personnel. In its assessment, OTA found that while intelligence agencies have confidence in the polygraph, there is little science to engender it. "The available research evidence does not establish the scientific validity of the polygraph test for personnel security screening. . . . OTA recognizes that NSA and CIA believe that the polygraph is a useful screening tool. However, OTA concluded that the available research evidence does not establish the scientific validity of the polygraph for this purpose."[9]

The report also cited two of the critics' ongoing concerns: the type I and type II errors I described earlier. Specifically, liars could learn to pass a polygraph and gain access to classified secrets, and truth tellers could fail and be falsely accused and penalized. "There is a legitimate concern that the use of polygraph tests for personnel security screening may be especially susceptible to: 1) countermeasures by persons trained to use physical movement, drugs, or other techniques to avoid detection as deceptive; and 2) false positive errors where innocent persons are incorrectly identified as deceptive."[10] Yet more than thirty years since that report was issued, the polygraph is still with us. In fact, it is often the polygraph examination that makes or breaks a clearance determination, placing individuals into a pass or fail category.

Kevin was born in another Western country but is now an American citizen. He lost his security clearance after failing a routine polygraph examination at the Department of Defense. He feels that the polygraph is still particularly important to the counterintelligence organizations for which he has worked for more than twenty years. He harkened back to another era in American history when describing the way the test was administered, the kind of people who administered it, and how they made him feel:

> They seem to be slaves to the polygraph, and it's odd that if they suspect you and you fail the polygraph, you have no hope . . . and there's been lots of evidence to expose the weakness of the polygraph, and the very high rate of false positives. But the counterintelligence community doesn't appear to have recognized this. . . . . I'm aware of all the abuses that occurred in the '50s, with the McCarthyist era, and I can imagine the mindset of the FBI counterintelligence people under Hoover. . . . But the attitude in the counterintelligence agencies that I was forced to, that I was abused by, and I include the FBI and DIA [Defense Intelligence Agency], was a shock to find out that this mentality still existed. Xenophobia, ignorance, arrogance, and bullying were prevalent.

Before failing a polygraph exam, Kevin shared the general public's perception of the polygraph: that if one fails the test, there must be a reason. "When I would hear about someone having a false polygraph, or a negative polygraph, I would always assume [there] was something behind it. You know, a normal, conservative person, and not knowing that much about it, I'd say, 'Well, [there] must be something there, if he's having security problems.'" Then, after news reports surfaced about his case, Kevin came under public scrutiny for failing an exam.

Kevin was surprised that the polygraph exam, having been scientifically discredited, carried as much weight as it did in the agency's decision to terminate his career there. His assumption was that, after twenty years of service, "the whole person" approach to security clearance adjudication would be applied to him. He had good reason for making that assumption, because the 2005 White House

revised guidelines for granting access to classified information specified that "The ultimate determination of whether the granting or
continuing of eligibility for a security clearance is clearly consistent
with the interests of national security must be an overall common
sense judgment based upon careful consideration of the following
guidelines, each of which is to be evaluated in the context of *the
whole person*" [italics added].[11]

But after failing the polygraph exam, no further discussion of
Kevin as a "whole person" ensued. He explained to me why this
surprised him so much. "Because, you know, we live conservatively,
well within our means, we pay our bills on time, no credit card
debts, alcohol abuse, all the usual things were absent that would
normally make a person vulnerable to spying or to exploitation by
a foreign intelligence service. None of those things were present, or
were ever present. And I assumed that that would come out, that
would be seen and evaluated and assessed. It wasn't. They didn't do
any follow-up. The polygraph was enough."

In 1985 the issue of using polygraphs exams on federal employees
came to the forefront of public debate when the Reagan administration and Congress battled over plans for expanding the government's
use of the polygraph. An executive order issued on March 11, 1983,
known as National Security Decision Directive 84, would have
sanctioned for the first time "adverse consequences" for a federal
employee who refused to take a polygraph test when asked. The
directive did not go into effect, partly because members of the Cabinet threatened to resign if it did. But the exam was quite common at
the time to deter what Reagan had termed "press leaks up the kazoo."

Bernie, a former executive at the Defense Department during the
Reagan administration, became embroiled in a leak investigation
at that time. He told me what happened to him when he passed a
polygraph exam and what happened to one of his colleagues who
did not:

> I gave a brief to the Defense Resources Board, basically, that
> said even with the Reagan buildup, we still had some shortages,
> and we need to think about it. Actually, it was written by a guy

working for me. So what happened was the *Washington Post* ran with it the next day. And of course the Democrats had a field day saying, "Oh, Reagan's spending all this money and things aren't getting any better." So guess who was suspect number one? Me, because I knew the reporter. And the thing that drove me nuts, well, I knew I didn't do it—when they told me to take a polygraph, I should've said, "Look, I'll take it to show you I didn't do it, but here's my resignation." That's what I should've done, looking back on it.

Bernie, like Kevin, was surprised that when an individual "fails" the polygraph exam, that person's entire record is overtaken by that one event. The "whole person approach" did not come into play. He was also surprised at the Pentagon's apparent readiness to fire or demote an individual with a proven track record of exemplary government service:

> Well, the interesting thing is, the guy who flunked the polygraph worked for me. He was the guy who wrote the brief. So he was a Silver Star winner in Vietnam, he was a West Point graduate, and the way they ask those questions, with the thing fluttering up or down and all that kind of stuff, that really bothered him, so the results didn't come out the way. . . . The reporter said that he wasn't the leaker, but they wanted me to fire the guy anyway. I told him, "I'm putting you on paid leave. Get yourself a good lawyer," because I didn't believe that he did it. And it turned out, they wanted me to transfer him to Defense Surplus Property Disposal Unit . . . or something, I said, "No, if you've got a case, make it," and of course they didn't, and he went on to have a very good career in the government. I think he just retired.

Unlike his employee, Bernie "passed" his exam, but not without difficulties. He describes the trepidation he felt answering questions and the consternation that his truth telling elicited from polygraphers during the process:

One of the questions, the guy says to me, "Have you ever cheated on a government form?" So I said yes, so then he starts, "What are you doing?!" all this kind of stuff. I said, "Come on, everybody exaggerates how much they give to charity on [their tax return]."

Years ago—people forget this—you used to be able to deduct cigarette tax and things like that, that they're never going to check on. We get through that. Then he says, "Other than that, have you ever done it?" I said, "Yeah." So we went through this whole long thing. When we deployed overseas, as typical government things, we got three dollars a day per diem. But if you were flying during a time when they gave you a boxed lunch, you could only get one dollar that day. So of course when we filled out our form, we [said we] never flew during lunchtime, so we'd get the maximum three dollars a day. Things like that.

Like Kevin, Bernie points to the discourse surrounding suspicion of a security violation, noting that even after being cleared, the stigma of being under suspicion remained. "In fact, everybody in my office thought that I had leaked the thing. So [when] I got back, I said, 'There's good news and bad news. The good news is I didn't leak; the bad news is they're going to go after me for cheating on my taxes.' And of course the guy did tell me, 'Whatever you say there can be used against you on these other questions.'"

The Presumption of Guilt

Brian held a top-secret clearance working for the intelligence community until he retired after twenty-four years of service. Every five years he was required to submit to a polygraph examination. He describes these exams as stressful, pointing out the power dynamic at work in the polygraph experience. "So your career depends on getting that clearance. You have to have it. So that really gives the clearance people, including polygraphers, a real strong upper hand because they're the ones who decide whether you're gonna have a job or not. So there's a lot of pressure on you there psychologically. There's just tremendous psychological pressure."

Brian enumerated some of the integral elements of the polygraph experience that lead to its stressful nature, including the adversarial posture of polygraphers. He noted that instead of presuming someone's innocence, they operated with the "presumption of guilt."

Now, I passed every polygraph I ever had, so I'm not one of these people who are saying, "Oh yeah, the polygraph is all screwed up." It was never a pleasant experience. It was always intrusive. . . . In a way, it was a bit demeaning. Because . . . when I first joined the agency, I had been in the Army for fourteen years. I was a combat vet. I had put my life on the line for my country. But when I went through that the first time, there's this sense of "You're bad, and I'm gonna find out what you did that's bad." And it didn't matter that I had done all this good stuff. It's like, "No, no, that doesn't matter. You're bad. You're sitting across from me and you're bad, and I'm gonna find it out. And maybe by the end of this, you might convince me that you're not." But there's the presumption of guilt.

Along with the presumption of guilt, some of those I interviewed used religious terms, describing, for example, the polygrapher's desire to elicit "atonement and confession." Brian describes the "incentive to cooperate" when the polygraph requires appeasement:

If you're in that position where it's like, "Oh, my God. I have to pass this thing." And they're telling you, "There's something wrong. There's something that keeps coming up." I think it would make a person disinclined to turn to the polygrapher or whoever is asking the questions and say, "No, there really isn't. I don't know why your machine is doing this, but there is nothing. I have not done anything wrong." Because you know that your job is on the line. So there is real strong incentive to cooperate. Your job's on the line. If you don't pass the polygraph, you don't get a job. If you don't pass the clearance process, you don't get a job. I would think any reasonable person realizes going into that, that you hold no cards; they hold all the cards. There's really no sense in arguing. . . . In my personal experience, I wrack my brain, and

I come up with a thing that, "Well, maybe it's this." And I tell 'em. So they formulate the question, and then they ask me. And then, after that, they will either say yes or no—you have satisfied the polygraph god. You have appeased the polygraph god. Or not, in which case you have to make another sacrifice. "Let me cough up this bit of information."

While it may seem outrageous that individuals submit false confessions in order to "pass" a polygraph exam, it makes sense in the context of what is at stake if they fail the exam. As Brian puts it, the odds are against anyone who does not appease the polygraph. "Obviously, you can always appeal the results of the clearance process. You can appeal. If you don't get your clearance, you can always say, 'What's the problem?' You can do that. . . . [But] I don't know anyone personally who has ever successfully appeal[ed] the results of the polygraph. I know of no one who ever did that and was successful, no one."

The government, in the early days of personnel security practice, relied in part on private security firms and organizations to assist with clearance practices. It still does, especially when it comes to the polygraph. It was during the 1950s that John Reid, a former Chicago policeman, developed a technique, using the polygraph, to elicit confessions. Today John E. Reid & Associates, Inc., trains more polygraph interrogators than any other company in the world. Reid & Associates' clients include police forces, the Department of Defense, the FBI, the CIA, and the Secret Service.

Critics have demonstrated that Reid-style interrogations, which detractors say use coercive techniques, can produce false confessions. Just as Brian felt compelled to "cough up" bits of information that polygraphers required as confessions, the Reid polygraphy interrogation technique, currently in use at the CIA and other government entities, is under scrutiny for having contributed to cases of "false confession."[12]

Clearly, polygraph examinations are administered by the government for government purposes. Andy describes the time, when his clearance was being revoked after a whistleblowing incident, he tried to take a polygraph in his own defense but was denied:

> You might find this ironic. I've never had a problem getting through the CI polygraph at DIA. I knew the guys very well. As a matter of fact, I would joke with 'em. It was like, "I'm ready. Put me on the friggin' box." When this all came up, Martha, I actually offered to do a polygraph. "You can polygraph me on the allegations. You'll find out that I didn't do anything wrong." . . . These were the things that were in my thinking. And I offered to take a polygraph on it. But they wouldn't allow me to take a polygraph.

Polygraph: A Failsafe in the System?

Many security professionals I spoke with readily acknowledge that the polygraph is not scientific. Rather they refer to the polygraph machine as the "box," a tool that should be used in concert with the other tools—interviews, investigations, and others to make determinations regarding clearances. Noting the flawed nature of the personnel security clearance process in general, and the dubious efficacy of the polygraph specifically, Karl, a Pentagon security administrator, says the polygraph, while not the scientific measure its proponents claim, serves another function. It gives a sense of comfort to those who need to believe that something scientific is being done. It gives the impression of a "failsafe" in the system, implying that the polygraph offers a kind of placebo effect for the insurmountable ailment of personnel security:

> My point about the polygraph . . . number one, the big idea that we have this apparatus, this personnel security clearance that's doing something, that gives people comfort. And then when you get down to the polygraph, whether or not it's really effective, there's this whole thing that this is really going to ratchet up, so squeeze these people down, and that's like the failsafe. . . .

Charles, the psychiatrist mentioned earlier, has his own theory about why good people get bad results from the polygraph:

My perspective is derived from my having seen people in the IC [intelligence community] for many years, mainly CIA . . . . I got a string of people that came to me who had "flunked" their poly. It was a very peculiar situation, because not one of the ones that I saw was a bad dude, not one. But they all shared probably one feature of their personality, namely they were obsessional and they were worriers, so that they got hung up on the poly, and even though they didn't do anything of any real consequence, that was enough for them to flunk the poly. Each time they tried it again, it got worse, and that had all the earmarks of what I've treated over the years so many times, namely phobias, phobic reaction. It was misinterpreted or led to confusion about how to interpret the results. Well, what would happen? "Well, the poly is only a tool." No, it is not. In the real world of the IC, if you get hung up on the poly, you're dead.

In addition to the technical difficulty of generating false positives for worriers, Charles put his finger on another underlying and persistent theme of several of the interviews: the fact that bureaucrats are risk averse. And that they never want to risk making a management or personnel decision that might harm their own reputations. They tend to protect themselves from scrutiny. "As you know, the default answer of any bureaucrat to anything is no, because it's safer for that person. If they say he's okay and something bad happens, it's on his watch, and who wants to risk that for their career?"

Even though the polygraph has been debunked by scientists, Charles points to another reason why the polygraph appeals to the personnel security clearance community. He says that it provides instrumentality to a process that is otherwise wholly dependent on human judgments:

It is an instrumental act. Why do surgeons make more than internists of all sorts? Because they do their thing, an operation or procedure, and [psychiatrists are] one of the least well paid of medical specialists. What procedures do we do? . . . All the rest of what they've got is all vaporware in a sense. It's talking to people, it's firsthand, secondhand, thirdhand information, rumor, innuendo. Fuzzy, amorphous, ambiguous. But with a poly, it's a thing, which involves an instrument. Now, we all know that the guy doing the poly and interpreting it is no more scientific than anything else. But at the end of the day, the polygraphist has to come up with an answer, either yes, no, or not sure, but they'll have to do it again. But in the end, they're going to have to come up with an answer, but even if the answer is ambiguous, that's also an answer, and the answer is bad. But think of how much having an instrumental intervention spares having to think. . . . Life presents so many decisions and choices. Isn't it nice when you can narrow it down so that you have one thing that either comes up yes or no, and you don't have to think? It does the thinking for you. So even though, like I say, they all say it—and I've heard it many times—"It's just another tool." No, you're using it like a pass/fail.

Tim, a security officer for a DoD agency, also expressed frustration with the intelligence community's dogged determination to maintain the polygraph program. In his opinion, other techniques, like one-on-one security reviews, are a better use of scarce resources and a better indicator of potential threats. Tim argues that personal, human interaction, on a regular basis between security officers and those employees assigned to them, is the best way to ascertain whether an employee has undergone experiences or personality changes that should lead to loss of clearance. According to Tim, such personal interaction gives the security officer the opportunity to ask pointed questions:

"How's everything going financially? Any debts that are bothering you?" which may shed light on potential issues before they erupt into security threats. I'm not a big fan of the polygraphs. I think they're a waste of money. I think if you took that money that was in the polygraphs and people that support it and you put it to do those annual reviews, you'll get a bigger hit on the people that are actually doing or are more subject to a possible threat of espionage or criminal activities. . . . You're gonna catch that. But polygraphs don't. Tell me what polygraphs stop.

Problems with "the Systems"

The government and private industry are working together to design IT systems that will further automate the personnel security clearance system. That work is both profitable and secret. This partnership of secrecy between the government and the defense industry goes on within the normative discourse surrounding national security but has a peculiarly commercial bent.

As a security executive, Karl also worries that, more and more, it is the defense industry and not the government that holds the reins when it comes to secrecy—and that the objective of national security may take a back seat to corporate profits. As a security professional working with the defense industry, he finds that defense companies are reluctant to admit when their systems have been hacked or infiltrated by foreign governments for fear of upsetting stockholders:

> And now we're even in a position, we see information being exfiltrated, but it's not [in] our mission set to be able to do anything about it. We can't tell industry directly. . . . Because even in the industrial base you have—like at Boeing, for instance, they have a great commercial business. If they're being attacked on the defense side, [we] can't make a big deal of that in public, because it might hurt their stocks. . . . But it's hard to change that culture, because as much as they want to, the CEO who wants to sell the Boeing 787s around the world, can't be saying to his shareholders that [the company is] leaking information, because it's being stolen from you out of your systems every day.

In 2013, the U.S. Justice Department indicted a group of Chinese hackers from the People's Liberation Army and charged them with stealing corporate secrets. But paradoxically it seems the harder the government and industry try to keep their secrets, the more unable they are to do so. For example, by designing an enterprise information system to process security clearance holders, the government and industry leave themselves open to new dangers posed by hackers of those systems.[13]

The ironic example of the hacker's infiltration of e-QIP, the U.S. Office of Personnel Management (OPM) system designed to collect information for the purpose of adjudicating security clearances, demonstrates the inherent vulnerability of systems. Charles notes that the government tends to fall back on the big-system approach to counter many of its problems. Having outlined the government's desire for the polygraph to scientifically remove human judgment from complex problems, he points to agencies' belief that IT systems can likewise cure what ails them.

> Yeah. I think they're working on these big systems. It's going to be about the data, the big data, and if all of these systems talk to each other—I heard that story—I've been in Washington since [the '70s]—I've heard this story so many times in different agencies that there's going to be a big solution, because this new system will finally override all these other legacy systems that are not talking with each other and blah, blah, blah. I can't think of one that has worked, that I've heard about. It's all—let's face it, big contractors, IT contractors, will sell the same story and literally hundreds of millions of dollars will be spent, and at the end of the day it's not accomplished. It's the FAA [Federal Aviation Administration], the FBI, I know of those. I heard a story about the CIA that there was a big area in the basement of the CIA that is filled with all kinds of legacy, very expensive, but now way OBE [overcome by events] equipment. That was one of these concepts that failed and they just tucked it under the edge of the carpet in the basement. All this machinery, and nobody wants to know or say anything about it. It's disappeared. . . . It's just not possible for such a thing to be made is what I'm thinking, in the real world.

I share Charles's concerns. I observed years of contractors "helping" the Department of Defense and the Department of Veterans Affairs to build an Integrated Electronic Health Record (iEHR) to provide a single electronic health record system for both departments, to no avail. I also worked for the Defense Department's Business Transformation Agency that pulled the plug on the

Defense Integrated Military Human Resources System (DIMHRS). That system was to have provided enterprise resource planning for the Army, Navy, and Air Force, replacing more than ninety legacy systems. The Pentagon killed it after spending more than ten years and a billion dollars on it.[14]

As Charles has observed in his Washington career, and in both of the above instances, private contractors convinced beleaguered federal agencies that technology was the answer to their problems. Then they proceeded to incur the kind of cost overruns for the government that would never be tolerated in the private sector.[15]

Problems with Leadership

Individuals who run afoul of the personnel security clearance system are often fired, demoted, warehoused, or otherwise removed from their careers and deprived of their livelihoods. Interviewees often complained about the lack of intervention on their behalf by managers, supervisors, and other officials who knew them and perhaps, because of their positions of authority, could have helped them maintain clearance. Bernie was a rare exception when he rejected the order to reassign his employee and instead advised him to find a good lawyer.

This failure of leadership is particularly evident when it comes during a whistleblowing incident—when an employee, by speaking out on a matter of conscience, embarrasses the bureaucracy, and runs up against the full force of government hostility and power. While the government espouses adherence to formal rules protecting whistleblowers,[16] it is not unusual for employees to lose a security clearance for having embarrassed government officials. As noted, the normative discourse surrounding the questions of personnel security clearance is so fixed and punitive that losing one's clearance is the beginning of the end for the accused, whether they are guilty of a security breach or not.

Andy related his experience testifying before Congress about the effects of whistleblowing on his career, noting that removing his security clearance was the first salvo of governmental reprisal.

He also observed that he is far from alone in such bureaucratic assaults:

> And I . . . actually testified. . . . That, you know, the security clearance system is used as a punitive measure of management's tools, rather than on trying to determine reliability. When I testified, there was a specialist right next to me, an E4 Army type, also in uniform. We talked about the fact what when he discovered wrongdoing regarding the Abu Ghraib interrogations and reported it, they took his clearance. Are you kidding me? The guy reports something that he's supposed to and they revoke his clearance? . . . Leadership, the way they use it, completely makes a mockery of it, because it makes it a punitive tool rather than a bellwether of reliability for the purposes of having access to national security information.

In describing the punitive nature of the actions against him and lamenting the lack of support from leadership, Frederick makes a distinction between the Marines he served with overseas and the Marines' support establishment in Washington:

> I'm extremely disappointed in the Marines that I have encountered. I'm disappointed in Marine Corps behavior off the frontline. And we call it the "support establishment." It means the Pentagon, Quantico, everything that goes on in the United States. The close ties of Marine generals to industry, to the extent that our commandant of the Marine Corps, who just left a couple of years ago, is now on the board of directors of Textron, a monster defense contractor who, if not already, certainly potentially will sell major programs to the Marine Corps. All of these ties are things that connect to what I reported. In other words, what I was reporting was all of that interconnectedness as well. And so instead of reflecting on themselves and saying, "Hey, wait, we're not behaving like Marines," they went after the messenger. "Shut [Frederick] up by any available means." And that's been disappointing.

Clearance, Identity, and Community

There are tremendous advantages to holding a security clearance, as Dana Priest and William Arkin have observed: "A top secret clearance is a passport to prosperity for life. Salaries for employees with top secret clearances are significantly higher than those for someone doing the same thing at an unclassified level. A clearance is also a guarantee of permanent employment, even in economic hard times. Top secret clearances are coveted for those reasons, and also because they are a sign of acceptance into an elite corps of individuals entrusted with knowing what other citizens cannot know, and with securing the country's future."[17] But as my interviews demonstrated, all of the financial security and prestige conferred by a clearance prove ephemeral the moment an individual falls through the cracks of the personnel security clearance system.

David is an attorney who specializes in whistleblower protection cases. He describes the situation in which individuals lose government positions and, with them, much of their sense of self:

> I think for a lot of people who have held clearances, it's very wrapped up in their professional identity. Whether it's because they're a government contractor or more likely because they were a member of the military, or possibly a member of the intelligence community, for them, having a clearance is kind of a badge of honor, and it means they're part of that community. And losing [it] oftentimes affects their sense of belonging and their sense of self-worth because they're no longer part of that community. They're not part of the tribe anymore. So if you cannot share in secrets, you're no longer part of the community. And that alienation is hard for individuals to take.

David stresses the fact that the loss of a clearance always has a traumatic effect on someone's identity and social self, even if the loss is not the result of the person's own actions. "Oh, yeah, this affects their life. It'll impact their social life, it impacts lots of things. Sure, it's livelihood, but there's a lot more to it. There's a significant degree of depression that will come for a lot of these folks, especially the folks that have been in the business for many, many years, and all of a sudden something happens." After decades of service, their trustworthiness is called into question.

Frederick, a whistleblower, falls easily into the category David describes. As a former Marine, he was a star performer on the fast track to bureaucratic success at the Pentagon before he came up for security reinvestigation for embarrassing his bosses by writing a report that outlined some of their failures. "Now, remember, I was a praised, popular guy before I [reported] those things.... So it was like falling off a cliff. I had just graduated. Right before I went to Iraq, I had just graduated from the Industrial College of the Armed Forces. They sent me to ICAF. I came back from Iraq with a recommendation to be considered for the SES [Senior Executive Service]."

Frederick's career came to a screeching halt because he identified and reported on misconduct by his superiors. He describes how his bosses, who were displeased with his behavior, managed to use his security clearance to sideline his career, even though he had committed no security infraction:

> But, hey, there's no forgiveness on certain things. And so, bam, off the cliff. So then I'm getting this reinvestigation during this period.... They sent me off for a polygraph because they were concerned. I wrote a paper at ICAF [Industrial College of the Armed Forces]. The subject was China. And in the process of this, I interviewed the number-three guy at the Chinese embassy. And all of this stuff was approved, of course, but when you get someone who's angry at you and they spin it in an interview—of course, that leads to these rabbit holes. So that was delayed. Readjudication was delayed for a long time. And as things progressively got worse with my situation ... then comes that fateful date where they said, "Okay, we don't trust you anymore. We're booting you outta here. We think you used a flash drive illegally in the SCIF [Sensitive Compartmented Information Facility]. We're stripping you of all your clearances and we're kicking you outta the Pentagon." Which they did.

Frederick described being ostracized, by members of the military with whom he had served and who had previously been collegial, as a result of the normative perception surrounding security clear-ance violations that "where there's smoke there's fire." After a story reporting his clearance revocation appeared in the local newspaper, he was surprised how quickly his professional community turned their collective back on him:

> I guess my primary concern about a reader is . . . well, everyone will parse an article apart; they'll find out the pieces they want. "Security violator" was the key point on me there. I guess I was—being brainwashed, I was worried about what my Marine Corps thought of me. Because the guys I'm surrounded by all these years in the Pentagon, who used to love me, all the way up to . . . the commandant of the Marine Corps retired me right there, under that tree. I had admirals in there. . . . All these people used to love me. And they spit me out like green mucus.

Despite the stress that accompanied his clearance revocation, Fred-erick tried to find meaningful work to do while the Pentagon kept him in clearance limbo. But as most know who have lived there for years, Washington can be a very small town. Frederick found that the rejection he had experienced by the military community in the national capital region was not limited to that geographic or organizational boundary:

> I tried to get other places around government. I kinda searched around during that bad year. I looked for congressional fellow-ships. I looked for anything where I could make a contribution, even a couple nonprofits—not government, nonprofits. And everyone pushed back on me and said, "Well, you know . . . while this whole thing is going on, it's kinda difficult." . . . You know what I mean, right? It's like, "No, because actually we don't trust you anymore either." That's how fast it happens. Or maybe they do, but they don't want the stigma. They don't want a guy who's having problems suddenly working for them. What does that look like? It's awful.

Doug, the former Marine and now attorney, represents clients in the intelligence community. He also mentioned the stigmatization his clients experience when clearance is revoked, noting the devastating effects of both the social stigma and the career ramifications of losing a clearance. The worst thing about losing a clearance? "It's like putting a 'T' for traitor on their professional chests. It not only will likely result in loss of current employment, but blacklisting for the rest of a specialist's professional life."

Laura, the longtime federal employee who married a foreign national, also felt she was wearing a letter of shame after she lost her clearance. She describes the feeling of isolation: "I really thought I was wearing a scarlet letter basically, and just so completely isolated, and that's one of the things that led to such a deep depression and anxiety. I have to tell you that I still suffer from anxiety periodically."

In David's practice as an attorney who specializes in whistleblower cases, he handles personnel cases for clients who work both in government and in the private sector. He says that while they may not be wearing scarlet letters, those government workers who have had a clearance revoked are uniquely and permanently marked. "So the process itself, I think, is uniquely traumatic. And then . . . the consequences are much more long term than a traditional termination. Normally, people have—very commonly, people have the option to resign rather than being fired, and that puts them on higher ground for starting over. Once your clearance has been suspended, unless you're exonerated, that mark's gonna follow you forever."

Jill describes her husband's loss of a friend, due to the rejection, stigma, and "guilt by association" that followed Jill's husband's loss of clearance. "His clearance was revoked after many years. One friend just put up a wall, because to continue association with him would have been to be tainted, or he thought it might taint him. That was very difficult. It was very difficult." As other subjects have noted, the mere accusation of a security breach is enough to endanger an individual's public reputation. In this case, risking a friendship with someone who had lost a clearance was too onerous. To maintain a friendship with someone who had lost his security clearance was to put one's own character in question and one's career at risk. Jill describes her husband's loss of the community with whom he had shared a sense of mission and a history. "These are the people that he built his life with, and to have it closed down was . . . and not be able to share the same things anymore, to have all those connections and all the respect and all the ability to make a difference taken away was very, very hard for him. . . . Once you're outside the family, you're outside the family."

Martin describes the particular and unique pain of those in the clandestine service who land on the wrong side of a security clearance adjudication. The power relationship between the state and the individual employee is particularly acute. A clandestine worker who is ousted from the government has virtually no résumé, no demonstrable work experience, no way to start over:

> Without a doubt, here in the intelligence world, in an agency such as DIA, CIA, NRO, NGA, orgs [organizations] like that, it's fundamental. If you don't have your access, whether it's suspended or revoked, you're out of the community. You're escorted out of the building; you can't get back in the building, you've gotta be escorted to go to the bathroom . . . those who are NOCs, nonofficial cover CIA, you lose your clearance, you've lost your entire identity. No one knows where you work, that you really worked for the U.S. government in the first place, and now you're completely on the outs. You're a pariah. You can't do anything with anybody. That's the worst situation.[18]

David has represented individuals who, when their clearance is revoked, are left to guess which of the guidelines they have transgressed. This can lead to personal feelings of loss and self-doubt. This practice seems particularly cruel and is key to the amorphous fear that disciplines those with clearances:

> All of a sudden, you've been a Marine for twenty-five years and had top-secret clearance, and you marry someone from another country, and they're an American citizen, but they have family members overseas. Your clearance is revoked, and they look at it as, well, you're [questioning] my trustworthiness. Which, realistically, they are, but technically, under that guideline, they're not. They're just doing a risk balancing, depending on

the country involved. It's not [questioning] the person's ... trust-worthiness. But clearances are always viewed as being attached to trustworthiness, because that's the determination. So they take it very, very personally.

Martin says that, when it comes to the circumstances under which individuals lose clearance, there is not much he has not seen. Although those whose clearance is revoked are hardly unique, the alienation and embarrassment that most of them feel makes them feel as if they are. They feel isolated, often convinced that they are alone and singular in their circumstances and feelings:

> And there's a huge embarrassment factor to it. So many of the clients, or, I'm sure, any of the lawyers that have it, we've seen it for so many years. There's nothing that surprises me anymore. I've pretty much heard it all. Every once in a while, there'll be something. I had a situation with a guy and a horse. Sorry. That was a little bit unusual, but that was, like, once in twenty years. Never had that happen again. Most of them are pretty much within the box of normalcy. You might not like it, it could be child porn, not stuff you really like, but it's seen it, done it—well, not done it, but that type of case, all the time. But to them, it's so unique, the person going through it, and they're so embar-rassed by it. Even if it's just ... a DUI. So there's a social stigma, absolutely, that attaches to it, someone who has lost a clearance like that.

Martin contrasts the offenses of child pornography and DUI to show the adjudicative spectrum. While an individual may not necessarily lose clearance for a single incident of driving while under the influ-ence of alcohol, he may find it harder to convince an adjudicative panel that he came into possession of child porn by mistake. As David also notes, adjudicators are people, and they have their own prejudices and predispositions. Some have alcoholic (ex-)spouses, and some have school-aged daughters and sons. It is unrealistic to assume that such personal characteristics do not come into play when adjudicative decisions are made.

Charles references the reluctance of bureaucrats to back down from a security clearance determination, even if it is questionable. "Because trying to get the thing reversed is very uphill, because it runs into all the things that we were talking about. It's just easier to just say no and keep saying no, because that's safer. Why do you ever want to admit you made a mistake in the first place? If you were the officer who denied the clearance, now you're going to say, 'Well, I changed my mind'? No, it's safer to just leave it alone, even if it ruins a person's career. I have several like that right now." Charles notes that in "some cases, there's some plausibility, let's call it. One could imagine that the IC would want to be more careful. Sure." But he finds that in most cases, removal of the clearance "made no sense at all":

> But I'll tell you, I know what the effect is. It's devastating to these men. Mostly, we're talking men. . . . That'll change over the years. But it's really like a castration. I've never said that before, but that's really what it is. The thing that defined them in terms of their identity has now been ruined. They used to be on the inside and now they've been shoved out, like an expulsion, being sent to Coventry. They are bewildered, usually for good reasons, because it makes no sense. They are hurt. They're angry, and they feel very defeated.

Left in Limbo

Geoffrey Bowker and Susan Starr examined the classification system in the South African apartheid regime. They observed that, in order to challenge the state's classification determination (as white, colored or Bantu), citizens would undergo a process that was constructed to adjudicate the cases. Whereas the apartheid system attempted to "create a normalized, systemic bookkeeping system embedded in a larger program of human destruction,"[19] the personal security clearance system's more banal focus is on suitability classification for government work. Yet there are similarities in the processes designed to adjudicate these determinations. One of those is the amount of time individuals were (or, in the case of security clearance, are) held in limbo waiting for adjudicators to determine their classification.

Bowker and Starr's work is instructive in the discussion of ethical concerns surrounding classification and bureaucratic procedures. One of their central arguments is that classification systems are often sites of political and social struggles, and that politically and socially charged agendas are often first presented as purely technical. "As layers of classification systems become enfolded into a working infrastructure, the original political intervention becomes more and more firmly entrenched. In many cases, this leads to a naturalization of the political category, through a process of convergence. It becomes taken for granted."[20]

Observations about the apartheid classification system mirror those described by government workers about their experience in the personnel security clearance system. Among them was what I call the "limbo factor." Megan describes the way her congressional staff colleagues had entered into limbo as, without a clearance, they lost their ability to function at the level required and eventually lost their jobs—unless the government has no case, in which case limbo can be eternal. "Eventually they lose their jobs because they can't perform at the level which they're assigned or graded, so their performance evaluations just basically show up as nonperforming. Then after a while they're fired. Or you have people sitting in positions and doing nothing for years and years and years, because the government basically won't deal with 'em."

Just as with the racial classifications of the apartheid era, security clearance determinations affect not only the individual being adjudicated but the entire family unit. Laura describes the emotional, psychic, and physical toll that more than a year in clearance limbo took on her, her family, and her home life:

Months passed. Months, with nothing, no information, no information. Months and months and months and months. So I started getting really depressed and really anxious. Seriously depressed, seriously anxious, and my husband and I started having marital issues, because he felt so, I guess, guilty, that I was having this huge problem . . . which of course, it wasn't his fault. . . . So our marriage started really just, I mean, going downhill. So we went to counseling. We both saw counselors. We both have prescriptions for antidepressants. It was really a very, very, very tough time, and we just—I had physical symptoms, like vomiting from the stress . . . so I've been like under this incredible stress to the point of a nervous breakdown. . . . Not eating, I lost so much weight. I was smoking like two packs of cigarettes a day. My husband and I didn't talk. It was just terrible.

After her seventeen-month wait in limbo, Laura received the agency's findings and was allowed to reply to them. After more limbo, the agency had apparently used the "whole person approach" to determine the good news: her clearance would be reinstated; the bad news: the government would dock her two weeks' pay as a punitive measure:

I finally get something in writing with their findings and their recommendation or whatever. When I got this, I didn't know what to do. I had an opportunity to respond, and so I did. . . . So I wrote this long thing—it took forever—and finally, I sent it off. Another three months of no response, and then finally . . . I got notification that they were not revoking my clearance, and I was being suspended for two weeks without pay, and that they took into account at that time my seventeen years of government service, my multiple details overseas, my outstanding evaluations, every year of government service, blah, blah, blah. . . .

Frederick spent his time in limbo under a kind of "house arrest." He could not report to work at the Pentagon. But he had to call there every morning:

So they sent me home on administrative leave for over a year. But they didn't stop paying me. I was very happy about that. My wife was very happy about that. But, yeah, it was a pretty scary time. So . . . I was on administrative leave and banned from the Pentagon. And every day I had to call in to my boss and report that I was . . . alive. By 8:00 in the morning, I had to call in, report that I'm here. I don't know what they were thinking. But that was the rule. And so I went through with that.

David has represented clients who have been terminated as a result of personnel security clearance actions and describes the stress that ensues as the limbo drags on:

> There's more emotional trauma and frustration than getting fired through the front door. The security clearance actions drag on a lot longer than a conventional termination. I remember one GAO study that people's clearances were suspended before they got to deciding whether to revoke them or not. But for an average of three years at the Department of Defense and the Department of Energy. So that's one factor that makes it more stressful and kinda drags out the misery. But then there's the additional stress of not knowing what you're accused of. Going for years where unknown charges that have the ugliest inferences and implications about them: possible traitor, not loyal enough to even look at important information to our country's defense. And you don't know why. There's nothing you can do about it. You're twisting in the wind for years.

According to Michael Herzfeld, time can be a "social weapon" for bureaucrats, warning that "time is a crucial component in concepts of the person." He observes that for individuals like those stuck in the limbo of a personnel security clearance investigation or adjudication the bureaucracy has the power to make time stand still. "By brusquely delaying action, a bureaucrat can deny the client's humanity."[21]

In his psychiatry practice, Charles sometimes treats cleared patients. He observes that even the best and brightest CIA officers do not stand a chance against the security clearance system if they have run afoul of it and the limbo factor sets in. "The system is built to defeat people. So what I saw is that some of these people were true national heroes—I'm talking about CIA officers—for what they did, the personal risk they took on and the lifetime of their career until this particular moment. And then what would happen is that they would go into an Alice in Wonderland zone; namely, they would no longer be qualified to go worldwide in their main job." Charles observes the deterioration of morale in individuals who, after having failed a polygraph, or under some other security cloud, are prohibited from going overseas—the kiss of death for careers in the clandestine service. By alienating these individuals, he said, and by placing them in security clearance limbo, the government may be doing more harm than good:

> Well, they weren't cleared. . . . However, they were allowed to stay stateside in the job that they were occupying. . . . So they were neither fish nor fowl. Their progression in their careers was completely halted, because they couldn't go out of the country and they couldn't get promoted for that reason. . . . So what happened is they were thrown into a state of anger, puzzlement, resentment, bitterness, and also forced mediocrity because what's the point of working hard if (a) you're not recognized; in fact, you're punished for it; (b) you have no more chances for promotion. Well, fine, I'll just run the meter until my retirement. So you take a decent officer and you convert that officer through this thing into the very thing you didn't want to have. . . . So it was very self-defeating on the part of the intelligence community to handle it that way, but it just evolved that way as a bureaucratic stupidity.

Laura echoes many of these same feelings; although her clearance was reinstated, she remains sour about the way she was treated. "So anyway, they suspended me for two weeks without pay, and this caused huge turmoil for us financially . . . but it was like, okay, thank you. Thank you for not firing me? I don't know, it was sort of like a—I was sort of bitter about the whole thing, because it's like . . . look how much time I paid for that in terms of emotional pain."

The financial hardship many experience in losing a clearance cannot be overstated, and it is the exceptional case when a clearance revocation has been successfully appealed. Such cases involve expensive legal battles that most federal employees and applicants are precluded from pursuing.[22] After the clearance is lost, it is particularly difficult for individuals to find employment in the national capital region. As David notes of his whistleblowing clients (whom he often represents pro bono), "What's the job market for national security professionals who lose their government jobs? Contractors?

You have to have a clearance to be a contractor." He points out that even if clients are exonerated the revocation appeals process takes so long to reverse that individuals no longer have the financial standing to obtain a clearance again:

> That's been a big concern, the sort of financial stability as a criterion, for whistleblowers who were fired, they lost their homes. They may, two or three years later, have won their appeals and got their jobs back, but they can't get a clearance because their credit got ruined during the interim. So it's another way to circumvent conventional legal remedies and rights that are exercised successfully, because you can say, "Well, during that period before vindication, they lost the necessary financial base to be trustworthy." . . . And that's not just hypothetical. I've had a number of clients that have just been terrified. Their cases are still pending. We're working our heads off to reverse those terminations and get them the vindication. They say, "What difference is it going to make? I lost my home. I went bankrupt. I'll never get a clearance again. And just by applying for a clearance, I'm going to be worse off than having been fired, because it'll be denied."

Kafkaesque Circumstances

Just as Charles described the Alice in Wonderland world that CIA workers enter when they are deemed "neither fish nor fowl," David describes the attributes his clients need to process as they enter the period of limbo. "It takes the rare exception to have stamina to stay strong during a process that typically has no deadlines, can drag on indefinitely. It's like Kafka's *The Trial*. That's the security clearance legal system, only it's not nightmare fiction; it's the facts of life for national security professionals." Using Frederick's case as an example, he notes that even with certain clearances reinstated, Frederick still could not really get back to work:

> In [Frederick's] case, it illustrates how protectoral the charges can be. In that case, the thumb drive the Marines charged him with using—they said, "We've got the serial numbers and everything. We can prove it." Then the manufacturer says, "There is not such

a numbering system for our thumb drives, so we don't know what you're talking about. But it wasn't from us." ... Now, luckily, the Office of Special Counsel acted based on everything surrounding the clearance, and their legal victory against all the surrounding circumstances was so impressive that the Marines dropped the clearance action. But ... it's not just the clearance. It's all the layers of security that are ancillary to the clearance. So he's got his clearance back, but he doesn't have access to the specialized compartmental information facilities, where the information is kept for him to use the clearance. He can't reach the document. If he could get there, he could read 'em. But he can't get there. And that's on indefinite delay. It could be years.

Another Kafkaesque aspect of living under the personnel security clearance system is the feeling of constant threat—of fear. Individuals succumb to an endless state of worry that they will somehow transgress the regulations of the system and end up losing a clearance. Part of the problem is that no one seems to know, exactly and fully, what constitutes such a transgression. When Hugh Gusterson interviewed government scientists, he found that this uncertainty considerably increased self-surveillance: "For example, one scientist told me that because of signs around the laboratory warning people not to discuss classified information on the telephone, she presumed, though she did not know for sure, that calls from within the laboratory were randomly monitored."[23]

Laura describes her experience as a state of constant worry and fear. "So my security clearance, it's always there, and one of the reasons is, of course, what exactly affects your ability to keep your clearance and how does that whole process work? The underlying thing is fear. It's fear if I lose my job, I'm going to live under a bridge with my children. What's going to happen to us? Fear, fear, fear, fear, fear."

Part of Laura's anxiety stems from the fact that she has been prescribed antidepressants and that the prescription could also affect her clearance. While she does not understand the underlying logic, she has heard from colleagues that a diagnosis of depression is a potential threat. "Well, because of course, if you're suffering from depression and anxiety, that makes you unstable and a risk to the security of this country. Hello. How? I have a coworker friend . . . who has suffered from depression, and he takes medications up the wazoo, but every time they're going to do that reinvestigation, he just goes into this frenzy of like, 'This time are they going to yank it? This time?'"

This fear may be partly reinforced through popular culture. In the first episode of the television series *Homeland*, Carrie Matheson, the CIA agent portrayed by Claire Danes, hides her mental health medications and keeps the fact that she is on medication from her government bosses. According to the *Homeland* website, "From the age of 22 she has been dealing with bipolar disorder, which is why she secretly takes an antipsychotic medication named clozapine."[24]

Medication may also be a lifesaver, however, for those who have lost a clearance. Doug described an incident when a client, after losing his clearance, attempted suicide in Doug's home. "I referred him to a psychiatrist . . . [because] that was more than a legal issue." Daniel, in describing the limbo effect on one of his clients, notes that having one's clearance revoked requires physical as well as mental resilience:

It's beyond feelings. It's physical. For example, one client, a woman . . . blew the whistle. She worked at the Department of Agriculture, never had any national security duties. She blew the whistle on spending the money for emergency planning to deal with natural disasters, like Katrina and other things like that, on junkets rather than serious emergency planning work. . . . She had her security clearance yanked. She was fired on the basis of having it yanked and got a good lawyer and he filed an EEO suit and got them to back off on the termination. So what they did instead, since her clearance was yanked and she wasn't trustworthy, is basically put her under professional house arrest. Reassigned her duty station to be her home and kept her there without any assignments for three years. She was a prisoner of her home. She would leave and they'd call. She'd be AWOL. The idea was to try and drive her crazy or something.

Another Kafkaesque aspect of the personnel security process is that individuals can lose clearance, or be ordered into an investigation, without knowing why. In Kafka's novel, the protagonist, K, is reminded by his lawyer that the proceedings are not public: "They can be made public if the court considers it necessary, but the Law does not insist upon it. . . . Under these conditions the defense is naturally placed in a very unfavorable and difficult position. But that too is intentional. For the defense is not actually countenanced by the Law, but only tolerated, and there is even some controversy as to whether the relevant passages of the Law can truly be construed to include even such tolerance."[25] Laura remembers trying to find out from her supervisor what "allegations of impropriety" had led to her being singled out for an investigation and interviews:

> I had put in for a detail for a deputy director assignment, and I was accepted and I was going to go on detail, and a week before I get an email saying, "We're sorry. You will not be able to go." No further explanation. I'm like, "Okay, this is really odd" . . . and by the way, I had gone to [another country], [and] I had gone to [yet another country] in the interim. So I had been on several other details . . . I got an email from OSI—Office of Security and Integrity—that they were going to come and interview me. With no further information. "Allegations of impropriety." . . . I have no idea what they're talking about.

One obvious aspect of federal workers' being confronted by the state and the personnel security clearance process is that they are also American citizens. It is bewildering to find oneself at the mercy of an institution that pays no attention to due process protections. Americans are used to being told that they have the basic right to know what charges are being made against them. It is unnerving for many to realize that they have largely signed those rights away by applying for a security clearance.

Kai Bird and Martin Sherwin describe Robert Oppenheimer's feelings when he learned, from his lawyer, the nature of the charges against him. The lawyer informed Oppenheimer that "the first step" of the review would be immediate suspension of his security clearance. Anne Wilson Marks did secretarial work for Oppenheimer in Los Alamos, New Mexico, where he led the Manhattan Project during World War II. Her husband, Herbert S. Marks, was a lawyer who eventually became general counsel to the Atomic Energy Commission. Anne remembered driving her husband and Oppenheimer to their Georgetown home one evening after the charges were made against Oppenheimer noting that, "on the way, Oppenheimer said, 'I can't believe what is happening to me.'"[26]

In Kafka's *Trial*, K's lawyer reminds him that, "in general the proceedings are kept secret not only from the public but from the accused as well. Only insofar as possible of course, but to a very large extent it does prove possible. For even the accused has no access to the court records, and it's very difficult to ascertain during the interrogations which documents are involved, particularly for the defendant who after all is timid and disconcerted, and distracted by all sorts of cares."[27] And indeed Bird and Sherwin reveal that government lawyers placed hidden microphones in Oppenheimer's lawyer's office that allowed the government, through transcripts provided, to monitor Oppenheimer's private conversations with his defense attorney. The FBI also wiretapped the telephones at Oppenheimer's home and in his office at Princeton. Oppenheimer and his counsel were never alerted to the fact that the government held (and made use of) these records during his security clearance hearing; nor were they even aware of their existence.[28]

Daniel describes an attempt to represent one of his clients at a security clearance hearing conducted by the Department of Homeland Security:

> As far as her due process rights, she had an hour hearing. She was not—they never told her what the charges were. We learned all these other things subsequently, after we went to the hearing. All we could do was sort of like give a eulogy for her. She couldn't present evidence. She couldn't present witnesses. She couldn't confront witnesses. The three people who were conducting the hearing, none of them made the decision. They were there to tape what her lawyers said, to be delivered to some other body who

would never meet her. And at the end of an hour, in the middle of a sentence, they said "Stop" and clicked the tape recorder. That was her due process.

Sometimes individuals never do find out what happened. Charles related that he is often baffled by agencies' decisions to remove clearance from his patients. "Now, I have worked with people who had clearances for a long time and then get them removed for this or that reason. In several cases . . . it's a total mystery."

Andy worries that this Kafkaesque nature of the national personnel security clearance system is damaging the nation it is set up to protect. His clearance has been reinstated since it was revoked, but only piecemeal for particular meetings and missions, when he was requested by the government to attend. He worries that such arbitrary removal of clearances from whistleblowers and others will come back to haunt us. "If the system holds no respect by those who live within it, what does that say about the ability of the state to maintain security safeguards? And it would be a shame if the government spent all the time and money that it does on the personnel security clearance system only to find that in the final analysis people rely on other mechanisms, like the 'old boy network.'"

After losing his security clearance for embarrassing his Defense Department superiors, to Andy's dismay he is still called into classified meetings within the intelligence community when his expertise is required, often obtaining an interim clearance for that purpose (or for that meeting):

It's been very fascinating, just sitting, doing what I do. In my next meeting, I'll be talking about nuclear weapons. It's not like the people I deal with have any less confidence in me based on the process, which is sad. If you set up a whole mechanism for establishing the reliability of someone and it becomes a joke, then people go back to what they always do: their gut. "I know you. I trust you. Therefore, I don't care what they say." And that's not the way the system should work. The system should reflect reality, not some . . . if you will, Seinfeldesque alternate universe that things are just completely out of sync with what really goes on.[29]

Brian felt that his experience with the personnel security clearance system, particularly the polygraph, had a "bizarro" quality that also ran counter to his sense of justice. Just as in Kafka's *In the Penal Colony*, where "guilt is never to be doubted," he found himself in the uncomfortable position of having to prove a negative.[30]

My problem isn't so much that we go through it, that we have to go through it. My displeasure is that I think it isn't done as well as it could be, and the focus is misplaced. That's my problem with the whole clearance process and obtaining clearances: The focus is misplaced. (1) There's an absolute over-reliance on the polygraph. (2) There seems to be an institutional mindset that you go into it with something wrong with you, that people who are interrogating you, "You did something, and I'm gonna find it out." And you may have done nothing, but it's incumbent upon you to prove that you're innocent. . . . It's a reversal of what we grow up with, what we learn: You're innocent until proven guilty. No, it's just the opposite. You're guilty until you can prove to them that you're not. You did something wrong, until you can convince them that you didn't, especially if that machine starts doing funny stuff. You are definitely guilty until you can prove that you didn't.

Self-Surveillance

The French philosopher Michele Foucault, in *Discipline and Punish*, outlines, among other things, the evolution of scientific methodology in state control of populations. In his discussion of Jeremy Bentham's Panopticon, a geometric design for prison surveillance, Foucault describes the efficacy of the apparatus. He explains that the Panopticon inures those observed to surveillance to the extent that they begin a routine of self-surveillance. The system removes the need for actual state control. Inmates essentially learn to police themselves. "The efficiency of power, its constraining force has, in a sense, passed over to the other side—to the side of its surface of application. He who is subjected to a field of visibility, and who knows it, assumes responsibility for the constraints of power; he makes them play spontaneously upon himself; he inscribes in himself the power relation in which he simultaneously plays both roles; he becomes the principle of his own subjection."[31]

Similarly, Frederick finds that government surveillance has changed the way that he looks at himself. He has begun to mirror the expectations of the personnel clearance system in his own self-assessments. While he admits the process of self-surveillance is "painful" he ultimately believes it is beneficial:

> What is wonderful about clearances and polygraphs and everything else is you have to painfully look in the mirror.... And, you know, that is healthy for any human being. And, sure, you end up living in a fishbowl, right? But you know what? I'm convinced you end up living a better life in many respects. You can't have a concealed life. It's very difficult to do.... I assume now, because I've been investigated so many times.... But I'm assuming at all times that my personal email and my phone are monitored.... I mean, this is an assumption, and it's a good assumption to go through life with.... If they wanna hear my dirty laundry business on the phone, that's fine. But it doesn't bother me. All I know is that there's no place to run. There's no place to hide and have hidden conversations. And it kinda feels good because . . . it just does. I don't know. That's been the way I've come to look at the world. By having nowhere to go and hide, it kind of stifles mischief in me, if you know what I mean. And I'm just saying, because I'm human, human nature, etc., etc. So something about the fishbowl that's okay.... It's a very positive thing. It's not necessarily.... I believe—this is more of a technology thing, but I believe the issue of privacy—you can forget about it. And don't try and hang onto it. You see how the society is desperately trying to hold onto privacy.... It's gone.

Karl is an administrator at a defense agency. He knows that he is under constant surveillance by the security clearance apparatus. But he also believes that the clearance system's constant surveillance of employees is helpful in keeping his own behavior in check:

> I think that I've been here long enough in my life, I personally believe that it's not the expectation that the system would fail me at this point; it would be me, for whatever reason, not upholding my responsibilities or accountability to the system . . . because I don't believe there's anything that's beyond any human being's ability to do under the right circumstances or conditions.

Surveillance is also on the minds of those who aspire to, but do not yet, work for the government. Kerry, a staff advisor to a congressional committee, finds that his potential choice of a government career curtailed his actions and behavior even before he applied for a government job. "I think there was some deterrent effect in knowing that adverse things showing up on your record could potentially jeopardize your ability to get a clearance. I will say that there were a lot of things I didn't do in school, knowing that this was a potential path for me and that I was thinking about government service and so didn't want to ruin the opportunity by having some type of blemish on my record that might prevent getting employment here."

Kerry does not say specifically which activities he avoided in his youth. He might have declined to smoke pot at a party, for example, in anticipation of a polygraph exam or other questioning around illegal drug use. But as Gusterson has observed, the self-surveillance that individuals experience around clearance can also constrain their sense of political agency and civic freedoms.[32]

Ron is a security professional in the intelligence community. During a discussion of the Obama administration's insider threat guidance to personnel to police each other, Ron expressed optimism that the new policy of peer surveillance could serve as a deterrent to leaking classified information. But he notes that such policies are in no way foolproof:

> One of the areas where the reform has helped some is this idea that you don't just go through the process once every five or ten years and then nobody bothers you again until it's time for

your next investigation. And the idea that someone is kind of looking over your shoulder all of the time, or the potential to have someone looking over your shoulder all the time, I think is much more of a—has the potential to be more of a deterrent. . . . Though, that being said, again, you can look back at these other examples, like Ames and Hanssen.

Laura, who had her clearance revoked and later reinstated, says she now "self-polices:" "It is just paranoia that's ingrained in you. I mean, honestly, I don't even have a clearance right now, because the position that I occupy right now doesn't require a clearance, but I'm my own clearance police. I have not changed how I behave [in] my job. I'm still, like I don't talk about it. Frankly, what I do is dry as toast." Like Kerry, Laura is thinking of future government work when she coaches her daughter in the art of "self-policing":

> My daughter . . . I've basically molded her into being a government employee [by telling her] "Be careful what you say, be careful what you do." . . . She actually did an internship with the government, and I'm pretty sure at some point she'll wind up working for the government because this is what she knows . . . and she totally gets it. Like you don't talk about stuff, you don't do stuff. . . . She has grown up that way . . . it's just ingrained. I'm not paranoid, I always monitor. The reason I got on Facebook was to monitor what my daughter was doing when she first went on Facebook, and guide her to the best of my ability through that process. So occasionally she would post some rant about somebody, and I'd be like "Nope. Gotta go, because if you ever want to work for the government, this can come back and haunt you." So I've taught her [to self-police] what you . . . post on Facebook, or any other media basically. So like I said, she knows she's being—she's been molded to be a government employee.

Consequences for the Family

Government workers are also family members. Laura explained how she is coaching her daughter to "self-police" in preparation for a government career. In most cases a loss of security affects the entire family. The benefits and sacrifices enjoyed and endured by government workers "spawn a tendency for the cleared not only to marry the cleared but to live around others with comparable restraints, gathered in neighborhoods populated by people like themselves in a version of a traditional military town."[33] One can understand why those with clearances would gravitate toward one another, particularly in light of what can happen to those who run afoul of adjudicative Guideline B: Foreign Influence and Guideline C: Foreign Preference. David's example of a Marine who lost his clearance for marrying an American citizen, but one with roots and relatives in another country, is instructive. This consideration poses a particularly grim problem for clearance holders.

Herzfeld and others have explained that nation-states must develop a certain amount of nationalism in order for bureaucracies to function within them. In many instances, uniting the citizenry against the Other by reminding them of family and blood ties to the state is effective —think about "Mother Russia" and Germany's "Fatherland." But because the United States is a nation of immigrants, the best we can muster is a "Homeland."

Jill, who held a security clearance in the intelligence community, describes some of the concerns her family had after her husband, who also worked for the government, lost his clearance. The loss of clearance, and subsequently his job, left the couple unsure how or if the incident would affect their children's future chance to enter government service:

> When we were debating about what to do about this when this was all happening. . . . We have . . . two kids in JROTC. One wound up going into the military. . . . There were unknowns. Is [their father's loss of his security clearance] going to affect their opportunities? And that was scary. So we talked about it as a family. . . . They believed in their dad, and they said, "Okay, we're sticking by you." But even with the risk of it affecting their lives and their career choices and what they wanted to do. So [there were] a bunch of unknowns. But daughter no. 2 has since received a secret security clearance, so that's a good thing.

Laura describes the financial and emotional effect that losing her clearance had on her home life. "My husband and I almost got a divorce over it. That's because he wound up having an affair after this whole thing was over, because I was so traumatized and so bitter about the whole thing. . . . So I wound up working a lot of overtime to make up for that time. . . . So we were separated for like a good three or four months, where he was not living in the house, was off with that woman." It is unclear whether Laura blames herself for her husband's affair. But she also conveyed the sad story of a colleague who stayed in an abusive marriage because she was afraid of losing a clearance:

> I had one coworker who was in this terrible, terrible, terrible marriage, and she could not, would not, leave because she . . . was going to wind up filing for bankruptcy, and she was afraid she was going to lose her job. So she stayed with this man . . . because she was afraid. I talked to her years and years about it, and—this is a long-term thing—finally she decided to leave him. She still has her job, so I don't know what happened, but can you imagine? You stay [with somebody] who's just downright abusive, and you stay because of your job? I don't think anybody should be put in a situation of such sacrifice for something that we don't even understand.

We don't know if Laura's friend would have lost her clearance for leaving her abusive husband. But we do know that security clearances are used by abusive husbands to intimidate wives. In 2014, Caitlin Gibson interviewed domestic violence victims' advocates for the *Washington Post*. Some were new to the Washington DC, area and the personnel security clearance system: "Right away, I noticed that I had victims with abusers who worked for the Department of Defense, for intelligence agencies, who were high-ranking in the military, all of whom had security clearances . . . I had to learn new ways of safety planning for them." Another counselor reported hearing "over and over again about an abuser telling the woman, 'If you report this, I will lose my clearance.' And given what the environment is now, that's not an idle threat. . . . Is he saying that to manipulate her? Yes. But he is also describing accurately what will happen if she has a valid complaint." According to Gibson, federal agencies are taking more seriously a history of domestic violence among cleared workers that, according to her sources, has noticeably increased in cases "where domestic violence constitutes grounds to revoke or deny a clearance."[34]

Domestic violence counselors new to the national capital area may be surprised by the cloak-and-dagger world that their clients inhabit, but they do not underestimate the extent to which wives and girlfriends fear the power, granted through a security clearance and access to classified information, afforded their partners. Siobhan Gorman, writing in 2013 for the *Wall Street Journal*, reported that NSA officers on several occasions had "channeled their agency's enormous eavesdropping power to spy on love interests."[35] Ryan Gallagher, reporting for *Slate*, details some of these encounters:

> One spy entered six email addresses used by an American ex-girlfriend into a surveillance system on the first day he gained access to it. He later claimed he had done so because he "wanted to practice" how to use the snooping technology. Another NSA spy monitored the phone calls of his foreign girlfriend for a month, claiming that he wanted to discover whether she was involved with any local government officials or any other activity that might get him in trouble. The worst punishment that was handed out in any of these cases was a reduction in pay for two months, a reduction in grade, and access to classified information being revoked.[36]

Gallagher's evident disappointment is that the worst punishment meted out by the NSA for these offenders was the revocation of access to classified information. What we know from this study (that Gallagher apparently does not) is that losing clearance is the beginning of the end for these government workers. They cannot function at the NSA without clearance. It is surely just a matter of time before that becomes evident—maybe not to Gallagher or the outside world, but almost certainly to those errant spies and their families.

Resilience, Dissent, and Disruption

There are ways to counter the domination exhibited in the personnel security clearance process that emerge from time to time. One way is to create communities to combat the sense of isolation that losing a clearance induces. For example, the Concerned Foreign Service Officers (CFSO) "is a group of current and former Foreign Service and Civil Service employees of the U.S. Department of State, created to investigate, document and expose alleged misuse of the security clearance process by the State Department's Diplomatic Security Service (DSS). CFSO's concern is the possibility that the clearance process can be used to circumvent Federal personnel regulations, to bypass equal employment opportunity laws and to punish dissenters and whistle blowers within the agency."[37]

Another way to challenge the system is to chronicle and publish one's experiences. Andy wrote a book about his experiences that ended up on the *New York Times* bestseller list. As required, he had submitted the manuscript to the Pentagon for review, and it had been approved. Despite that fact, the Pentagon claimed that Andy had revealed classified information and ordered all the copies pulled from local bookstores and destroyed. In addition, the Department of Defense threatened Andy and his publisher with legal action. Not surprisingly, these events generated attention and interest in the book, infuriating the Defense Department while putting money in Andy's pocket. After resubmitting the book to Pentagon censors, Andy's publisher came out with a revised and redacted version, titillating new readers and rendering the original copy a collector's item. Ironically, he determined that the more punitive the measures the bureaucracy used to suppress him, the better it was for sales.

> This is the grand irony. . . . The one thing that is most difficult for a clandestine operative to have is legitimacy, is for the government to say, "Yeah, he was really clandestine.". . . Because if I went to a publisher and said, "I did all this." Like, "Oh yeah, sure you did." . . . So it's great for sales. It's great. . . . They made it a bestseller. . . . They gave me legitimacy, where if they had just

said, "We don't know who this guy is. We don't know why he's doing this. Yeah, he had a clearance at one point in time, but a lot of people have clearances." . . . And then leadership backed 'em up. The leadership should've said, "Stop this. This is just insane." Instead, they backed up their bureaucrats and then they doubled down on stupid and it's gotten worse. It's kind of like they helped make me who I am by being so mean about it. So I just take it in stride.

Andy's experience points to the possibility that the personnel security clearance system and the national security state may be largely to blame for many of its own crises. Often the state's misdeeds are concealed behind the finger-pointing and demonization of individuals within the system. When everyone is looking at the bad guy who has had his clearance removed, nobody is looking at the bad system that granted the clearance and then took it away.

Sadly, bestselling authors are the exception to the rule among those who lose a security clearance. Most individuals who lose a clearance lose friends and livelihoods. They experience isolation, depression, and family upheavals that can last forever. Although Jill is still a government supervisor, she is now reluctant to recommend government service to young people after her husband lost his clearance:

And how do you even bring new people into that process when it's so, I mean, it can destroy your life? . . . And you want to be able to say it's a just and fair process, and everything is going to be okay. Because they're going to put their whole lives on the line, saying, "Okay, take a look at me, this is what I want to do." But if the look is taken and the rejection is made, they've lost everything. That was one of the hardest things for me . . . being able to be continually supportive of the process . . . as we're still living the victimization of what it cost us.

Laura, in summing up her experience of losing her clearance, echoes many interviewees' experiences and feelings about the need to improve the system:

I love my job, and I love the government. That's one of the things that . . . hurt me so much about this whole thing. I mean, I'm like the last person that would ever do anything to hurt this country or my government, but they treated me like a criminal. And despite all of that, I'm still rah, rah. I think people like me just go quietly off into the sunset and never complain, never do anything. I would never dream of doing anything that would cause anybody harm. I have no respect for people like Manning and Snowden and all those people, because to me there's some sort of element of ego, and it's not—whatever they may think that they're saving the United States from, the damage that they cause is so much greater. . . . They do need to have a system in place that is more transparent, and I think that would make it easier to ferret out your Snowdens and your Mannings and all those people. The way their system is set up now unnecessarily and unfairly targets people who've not really done anything in the overall scheme of things that will harm the security of this country, but they're so focused on those, they divert their resources to that, instead of dealing with their problems that are right in front of them. No one like Snowden should have access to so much information. No one.

Thoughts on Puritanism

Max Weber, in *The Protestant Ethic and the Spirit of Capitalism*, recounts how Puritanism became entwined with the virtue of labor. He examines the writings of Benjamin Franklin and Franklin's Calvinist father, who was responsible for many of Franklin's ideas, among them being "called" to a specific profession.

Jill describes what her husband felt when he lost his clearance in terms that Weber and Franklin would understand. She said that her husband had lost what he had been "called" to do. "It was everything that he had ever worked for, everything he ever believed in. To him . . . he considered what he was doing a calling. And to be denied that is just to change your whole person. That's who he was through and through and through and through. And so to have all that invalidated, or not believed . . . was hideous as a human being."

Weber argues that ascetic Protestantism was one of the major "elective affinities" in determining the rise of capitalism, bureaucracy, and the nation-state.[38] The binary nature of relationships of Western Puritan thought—good versus evil, truth versus lies, with us or against us—in the security clearance process and in the imaginations of those who monitor and are monitored by the system is worth exploring.

Herzfeld explains how Western bureaucracies treat rationality as distinct from belief, yet demand an unquestioning faith not radically different from that exacted by some religions. "Even critics of the state bureaucracy implicitly accept its idealized self-presentation. The nation-state represents perfect order; only the human actors are flawed. This has all the marks of a religious doctrine."[39] Many interviewees described being made to feel "bad" during security investigations and "good" once the process was finished. Brian describes his experience with the system, and particularly the polygraph exam, as a "cleansing":

It seems that there's almost a mindset that the degree to which we can make it difficult and egregious and unpleasant is commensurate with how successful we feel we've cleared you . . . . It was my personal experience that there's a mindset that if we can make the clearance process as unpleasant as possible, in the end, we will have a better person. We'll have done our job better. . . . When you first clear the person, if you make it as difficult and unpleasant as possible, the end product is a person who you feel pretty good about. You feel like you have done your job well if it's lengthy and fairly unpleasant. . . . But somehow . . . at the end of this lengthy clearance process, you're cleaner. You're cleaner for having gone through this. . . . There's an unconscious belief that the more unpleasant you make it, the more likely somebody is to come out and say something that they did—and there might be some truth to that. . . . You have helped forge them by having put them through the process. You have contributed to making that person better at whatever it is that they're going to do in the future. That was just my impression. It just seemed harder than it had to be. It seemed more difficult than it had to be, and sometimes more difficult than reasonable. All with the mindset that if we do it completely thoroughly, if we give them the Spanish Inquisition, at the end, they're so clean that we can go for however many years before we do them again, before we cleanse them again. You're through the cleansing process, and then you're clean. And years can pass before you have to be cleansed again.

But, as many interviewees pointed out, it is impossible to corral human beings into the "good" and "bad" categories required by the personnel security clearance process. William, another attorney who specializes in whistleblower cases, acknowledges the "good–bad" binary may not work when it comes to human beings. There are too many gray areas.

I actually don't care for the term whistleblower because it is a loaded word, it seems to me. When somebody says I am a whistle-blower, they're saying what I revealed is injustice, and the people I revealed it on are the people who committed the injustice . . . you're already telling me that you're right and the other guy's wrong. And I rebel against that sort of heavy-handedness. I resist it because it is a loaded term. Now, it doesn't mean it's never appropriate. There are people who have taken profound risks as acts of conscience to expose wrongdoing. And in fairness, the term is recognized in law. The Whistleblower Protection Act uses the term whistleblower, so the term is recognized. But exactly who qualifies and what does it mean is a little bit complicated. I think one can be a whistleblower and still have engaged in wrongdoing. One can be a whistleblower and violate a nondis-closure agreement. One can be a whistleblower and still be kind of a bad guy. Life is complicated. So if you acknowledge all of those nuances, then it's possible to have a conversation. If it's a bid for "look at me, I'm a hero," then that creates skepticism in me.

As William notes, human behavior is nuanced and complex. There are shades of gray in individual behaviors just as there are in the behavior of the state. Yet there is little motivation, on the part of the state, to interrogate itself as thoroughly as it does those who run afoul of the system.

The binary between good and bad obfuscates the great variety of dangers posed by spies, leakers, and others. It leads to the quest for quick fixes and leaves unexamined the ways the bureaucracy has exacerbated dangers through ineptitude, negligence, malice, prejudice, and magical thinking. As Edward Shils reminds us, "Since lunacy cannot be entirely eliminated, those who share responsibility for conducting our affairs must not form alliances with it."[40]

4 Recommendations for a Better Personnel Security Clearance System

Throughout its history the national personnel security clearance system has been shrouded in secrecy. By definition, secrecy precludes open discussion of the process. Thus, one who finds fault with the system may be deemed by some as untrustworthy simply by doing so. Because the system is about secrets, open discussion is discouraged. But discussion is precisely what is needed in order to improve the system.

In chapter 1, I noted that there is a tendency for national security bureaucracies to outgrow their scale of need. During the Lavender and Red Scares, reasonable security measures slid into paranoia. In chapter 2, I described the personnel security clearance process and how it sometimes goes awry, demonstrating, for example, how urinalyses and polygraph exams can produce both false positives and false negatives. Nevertheless, the personnel security clearance system often functions exactly as it should. Some candidates are rejected for just cause. Some clearance investigations reveal and remove threats. But as the experiences of my interviewees demonstrated in chapter 3, the system is also used as a blunt instrument against those who speak truth to power.

Although the system is designed to help keep our nation safe, and I believe that such a system is necessary and important, it has some serious flaws. Having pointed out some of its weaknesses, I am now obligated to suggest how to make it work better. The narratives of those I interviewed, who have suffered the consequences of this flawed system, have led me to develop the following recommendations for improving the personnel security clearance process.

Recommendation: Guard Against Prejudice

The observation by Geoffrey Bowker and Susan Starr that classification systems are often sites of politically and socially charged agendas is important. I have shown that agendas are often first presented as purely technical.[1] The technical approach to eliminating the LGBT community from federal service during the Lavender Scare is one example of how a political intervention can become routinized. The rationale for the removal of gays and lesbians from national security jobs was that they were uniquely susceptible to blackmail. That premise was untested, yet it went unchallenged.

The FBI's 2002 Post-Adjudication Risk Management Plan, or PARM, singles out for additional surveillance hundreds of FBI employees who were born overseas or have connections there, ostensibly to prevent foreign spies from coercing them to betray their country. One way to mitigate actual security risks is to reassess the assumptions underlying programs like PARM. Just as the authorities were wrong about the LGBT community during the Lavender Scare, they have been wildly wrong in the past about who poses a national security risk. In the quest for security, a nation of immigrants must rely on the better angels of our nature and reject, rather than perpetuate, xenophobic predispositions.

In the case of the FBI's PARM program, the government may be working against its best interests. The United States needs diverse and talented employees. A January 2013 report to the president and the Congress by the U.S. Merit Systems Protection Board states that employees of the federal government and applicants for employment should receive fair and equitable treatment in all aspects of personnel management "without regard to political affiliation, race, color, religion, national origin, sex, marital status, age, or handicapping condition, and with proper regard for their privacy and constitutional rights."[2] It is counterproductive to risk losing individuals with specific and vital skill sets by singling them out because of the very characteristics they were hired to possess, such as languages and regional and cultural familiarity.

Bureaucrats should have learned from the wrongs committed against Americans of Japanese descent during World War II and during the Cold War's Red and Lavender Scares not to single out groups of citizens and employees for disparate treatment. Nathaniel Frank tells how the combination of homophobia and xenophobic policies hobbled U.S. foreign policy and security objectives, specifically through the "Don't Ask, Don't Tell" policy during the Clinton and Bush administrations: "The story of the ongoing purges of gay soldiers, sailors, airmen and marines with language skills critical to waging the war on terrorism pits political expediency and moral dogma against national security. . . . It is a story that shines a spotlight on certain truisms that Americans seem to grasp only when it's too late, and then to promptly forget until the next time it's too late: that prejudice is generally self-defeating rather than productive, and that it nearly always has unexpected consequences."[3]

Such consequences are, as often as not, undesirable. Sam Sieber points out that when the state overreaches it creates the possibility of its own interventions being exploited "in a manner that subverts or even reverses an intended outcome." Sieber observes that "the theft of military secrets is, of course, a common and by now thoroughly predictable case of having one's weapons turned against oneself. This pattern is not restricted to warfare, hot or cold, moreover, but may occur in any hostile relationship."[4]

If federal agencies want to enhance national security, they must reconsider programs that single out subgroups of employees for disparate treatment. Instead of alienating specific groups of federal workers, or making their work more onerous, we need to work together to improve the security clearance process overall.

Recommendation: Beware the "Chutzpah" of Government Retaliation

It would be helpful if bureaucrats were made aware of and encouraged to resist patterns of behavior associated with the revocation of clearances. This is particularly true in their treatment of whistleblowers. The tendency for the bureaucracy to "blame the victim" in whistleblowing incidents results in retaliation and counterattacks on an individual's character.

That some government appointees behave this way is not surprising. Some hail from political campaigns, where smearing one's opponent is de rigueur. But it is more distressing when conducted by career civil servants who ought to know better. Such bureaucrats are often actually employed to preclude such abuses from happening. In one particularly shocking example the agency charged with protecting whistleblowers, the U.S. Merit Systems Protection Board, retaliated against its own in-house whistleblower.[5]

Removing (or "pulling") a clearance is often just the first salvo in the arsenal of government retaliation. David, an attorney who represents whistleblowers and is familiar with the tactics used against them, describes state action against whistleblowing employees as "common and toxic." He mentions a few of their "kneejerk reactions": "One is to pull their clearance, to isolate them. The second . . . is to pull their clearance to discredit their dissent. Usually, the national security whistleblowers . . . are going to run headlong into a subjective conflict of interest, a personal conflict of interest, where someone who's buried in the middle of the chain of command is gonna get in a lot of trouble for blowing it. And their personal ambitions or desire to avoid accountability become a conflict of interest with the institutional mission." David describes having seen this scenario unfold time and again, pointing out what he calls "the classic tactics of retaliation":

> One of them is to isolate the whistleblower by cutting them off from access to information. The other is what we call "chutzpah" in making the charges. Whatever the employee is blowing the whistle on, you accuse them of that misconduct, and usually an uglier version of that misconduct. So if someone is blowing the whistle on sexual harassment, they'll be fired for sexual harassment. If somebody is blowing the whistle on a security breakdown, they'll get their clearance yanked for being a security threat. It's very Orwellian. It's very effective. It's the most

comprehensive way to attack someone's credibility. And it's sort of a subset of another classic retaliation tactic that's really the first principle. I called it "the smokescreen syndrome." It's to shift the spotlight from the message to the messenger. So the first reaction to whistleblowing typically is, "We need some dirt on him." Open up a retaliatory investigation. It's the larger version of discrediting the messenger. The more surgical version of it is "smear them with the same alleged misconduct that they're challenging."

By using such smear tactics, the state shifts the focus of the discussion onto the employee and away from the real problem that the employee has identified. Smear tactics are designed both to distract and to discredit. As David sees it, one reason the government can act with impunity is because there is so little transparency inherent in the clearance process:

> You can't take anything this person says seriously. Security clearance retaliation is uniquely susceptible to that type of cheap shot because, depending on the agency—in all agencies, to an unprecedented degree—you don't have to defend your attacks. The employee doesn't even necessarily get to know the specifics that he or she is charged with, let alone confront their accusers or do discovery. You can avoid all the muss and fuss of due process or constitutional rights and have the ugliest possible smear that, due to its lack of specificity, is even scarier to discredit than someone who's challenging a legitimate problem. So it's been a very, very effective tactic to use against national security whistle-blowers. It's like a free ride for harassment.

Interviewees' experiences point to the possibility that the personnel security clearance system may be largely to blame for many of its own crises. When the state seeks to hide its misdeeds behind the finger-pointing and demonization of individuals in the system, everyone loses. When everyone is looking at the bad guy who has had his clearance removed, nobody is looking at the bad system that granted it and then took it away.

Recommendation: Be Fair and Aim Carefully

Megan, while working on a committee staff on Capitol Hill, has seen her share of colleagues lose clearance. She notes that many of those clearances were lost not because of security concerns, but because of whistleblowing or other embarrassments to committees or individual members. Federal managers should be careful to differentiate between infractions of security protocols, which justify pulling a clearance, and other infractions that do not:

> I think where some unfairness probably comes in is when clearances are pulled without sufficient documentation, or pulled for less than security reasons. That is a very sharp, a very heavy weapon that an agency holds over a person. It basically can affect their whole livelihood. All the hoops that have to be jumped through to get it back, it's basically a "guilty until proven innocent" situation, as opposed to the other way around, which is what the Constitution is supposed to allow us. The onus is on you to prove your innocence as opposed to the onus being on the state to prove your guilt in this system.

Doug, an attorney who represents federal employees, explains that the removal of a clearance is often much easier for federal managers than the standard procedures for terminating employees for cause:

> The SOP [standard operating procedure] is . . . the back doorway to fire somebody without the muss and fuss of legal rights. And that means that it's uniquely susceptible to hidden agendas. On my beat it's whistleblower retaliation, but [for] other folks, [it's] religious discrimination or race or sex discrimination or buddy system agendas. "I wanna get rid of somebody so I can get my own guy in there." There are so many ways that it can be misused. It's become—well, its official and legitimate purpose is a safeguard for the reliability, the trustworthiness of those who work with classified materials. In practice, because of the lack of checks and balances, it's a shield to accountability for illegal hidden agendas. And that's why this is a real problem.

David sympathizes with federal workers who are in limbo: They've had a clearance removed but haven't been fired. "Yeah, I think that is the worst. I think there's also a lot of—there's more emotional trauma and frustration than getting fired through the front door. The security clearance actions drag on a lot longer than a conventional termination." It may be easier for federal managers to warehouse an employee, by pulling his or her clearance, than to account administratively for why an employee should be fired. But it is certainly not easy on the employee.

Doug has seen many cases in which managers fail to consider the long-term ramifications of suspending a clearance on an employee's career: "So the process itself, I think, is uniquely traumatic. And then, as I said, the consequences are much more long term than a traditional termination. Normally, people [in other jobs and industries] . . . have the option to resign rather than being fired, and that puts them on higher ground for starting over. Once your clearance has been suspended, unless you're exonerated, that mark's gonna follow you forever."

Agency managers should never pull a clearance arbitrarily just because they want someone fired. If a manager wants to remove an employee, there are mechanisms in place to make that happen. Pulling a clearance arbitrarily or unjustly is lazy and harmful and can ruin a federal career.

Recommendation: Consider Due Process

As Megan has observed, an individual whose employer has removed her clearance is "basically guilty until proven innocent." Doug, an attorney, points to the propensity of federal agencies to drag their heels during clearance hearings and adjudication processes. He says that for the state, such stall tactics sometimes make the problem go away. When the employee runs out of money for a legal defense, or just plain loses patience, he or she will go away. "Frankly, [it is] bullshit, but I had to go through the process and it is so lengthy and punitive. Because of the length of time. I have lots of CIA cases, but there's just no way . . . that it takes that period of time, a year and a half to two years, to go through the . . . procedures. It's just ridiculous."

David has observed that many employees stop contesting a security clearance decision because they have been both financially and emotionally exhausted by the process. "It takes the rare exception to have stamina to stay strong during a process that typically has no deadlines and can drag on indefinitely. It's like Kafka's *The Trial*. That's the security clearance legal system, only it's not nightmare fiction. It's the facts of life for national security professionals."

For federal workers preparing to defend themselves against clearance revocation, perhaps the most helpful improvement to the procedures would be to inform them why the action has been taken in the first place. And it would also be helpful to put a time limit on the appeal process. As David, who has witnessed many such cases, puts it, "There's the additional stress of not knowing what you're accused of. Going for years where unknown charges that have the ugliest inferences and implications about them: possible traitor, not loyal enough to even look at important information to our country's defense. And you don't know why. There's nothing you can do about it. You're twisting in the wind for years."

A subset of this recommendation to consider due process is to "drop the box." By this I mean discontinue polygraph testing for personnel security clearance screening. Both the Office of Technology Assessment of the U.S. Congress and the National Academy of Sciences have debunked the polygraph's claim to scientific lie detection. In addition to the unscientific nature of the device, the Reid-style interrogations discussed in chapter 2, used by the CIA and other agencies' polygraph programs, have been demonstrated by critics to produce false confessions. The U.S. Supreme Court has determined that polygraph tests can be banned from courtrooms. Justice Clarence Thomas wrote for the court in a decision, "There is simply no consensus that polygraph evidence is reliable."[6]

Recommendation: Use Technology, But Do Not Rely On It

Andrew Katz, writing for *Time* magazine after the Edward Snowden leaks on NSA programs, noted that college campuses routinely check applicants' online presence, while federal clearance investigators do not. I believe that the personnel clearance investigative process should include a review of applicants' and employees' online profiles and social media. "Just days after Snowden's unveiling, snippets from more than a decade of his online history were uncovered that could have been cause for investigators' concerns. . . . Ironically, the government might be able to prevent leaks like the one that revealed a widespread Internet surveillance program if they do a little more online detective work . . . it appears that college recruiters look more rigorously at applicants' online lives than some federal departments."[7] Though it appears there may now be some progress on this front. On May 12, 2016 the Office of the Director of National Intelligence (ODNI) issued SEAD 5, "Collection, Use, and Retention of Publicly Available Social Media Information in Personnel Security Background Investigations and Adjudications." The *Washington Post* reported the government will start scanning Facebook, Twitter, Instagram and other social media accounts of thousands of federal employees and contractors applying and re-applying for security clearances using this "first-ever policy."[8]

Doug, an attorney who represents federal clients, also recommended using online information to vet those seeking clearance. "What they should be doing is checking out your Facebook feeds and your LinkedIn and your activities online. Is a Google search even part of the security clearance process? It should be, right? You're gonna learn more running someone through Google, People123, and Spokeo than you will by . . . asking their neighbor."

Andy, who lost a clearance after twenty years at the Department of Defense, wished the investigators had interviewed a wider array of his acquaintances—people who knew him well, unlike his neighbors—and had made better use of social media:

The . . . thing that obviously I think they don't do enough of is talk—for example, the people I work with, or the people I both served in combat with or I've known for thirty years, some of the people on my Facebook, for example, I would have no problem with people looking at my Facebook. . . . If there's things regarding my reliability, I have no problem with people looking at my Facebook. . . . Not your neighbors. Like, "Hey, is he a good guy?

Does he put his Christmas lights up on a timely basis and take 'em down before January 15th?" It's insane.

Although it might be prudent to use existing Internet technologies for investigative purposes, it would be less prudent to rely only on promised future technologies, like the Personality Disorders Security and Safety Risk tool anticipated by PERSEREC. When making determinations about human behavior, human beings should be kept in the loop. One could argue that the task of security clearance adjudication is inherently human. Building an algorithm that can make such determinations on its own may not be possible. Also, reliance on technology can sometimes backfire. The development of an algorithm or machine that can detect and predict current and future human frailties and proclivities is dubious. And if a technology makes those claims, it may create a false sense of security.

To illustrate the need for caution in the use of technology, we can look at the problem of hackers who target government systems.[9] They have gained access to e-QIP, the system designed to collect information for the purpose of adjudicating security clearances. The Office of Personnel Management has determined that hackers are now in possession of the social security numbers and other personally identifiable data of thousands of government workers. So it is becoming clear that IT systems come with their own built-in set of problems.

As Charles, the psychiatrist, so eloquently notes, the government tends to fall back on the big-system approach to counter many of its problems. But big systems take time to build and are expensive. So federal managers should consider carefully the costs and benefits associated with them:

> I think they're working on these big systems. It's going to be about the data, the big data, and if all of these systems talk to each other. . . . I've heard this story so many times in different agencies that there's going to be a big solution, because this new system will finally override all these other legacy systems that are not talking with each other and blah, blah, blah. I can't think of one that has worked, that I've heard about. . . . Let's face it, big

contractors, IT contractors, will sell the same story and literally hundreds of millions of dollars will be spent, and at the end of the day, it's not accomplished.

Secretary of Defense Robert Gates made similar observations in 2010 when testifying on Capitol Hill about the planned Defense Integrated Military Human Resources System (DIMHRS). That system was to provide joint pay and personnel services to the Army, Navy, and Air Force, replacing more than ninety legacy systems. The Pentagon finally killed the project after spending more than ten years and a billion dollars on it. A sad footnote is that even the secretary of defense did not fully understand how much the debacle had cost taxpayers: "'I would say that what we've gotten for a half billion dollars is an unpronounceable acronym,' Gates quipped, though his cost estimate was short by half. The Government Accountability Office says a billion dollars had been spent on DIMHRS through 2009."[10]

Recommendation: Reduce the Number of Clearances

As of October 2014, according to the director for national intelligence, the number of persons eligible for access to classified information was 4,514,576.[11] Committees and working groups have long counseled that a way to improve the system is to make it smaller. In 1997, for example, Senator Patrick Moynihan's Commission on Protecting and Reducing Government Secrecy recommended, "The best way to ensure that secrecy is respected, and that the most important secrets remain secret, is for secrecy to be returned to its limited but necessary role. Secrets can be protected more effectively if secrecy is reduced overall."[12]

After the shooting at the Washington Navy Yard in September 2013, the Congressional Committee on Government Oversight conducted a hearing on the security clearance process. The consensus at the time was that too many clearances had been granted. "Far too many people have security clearances," is what former assistant secretary of defense for homeland security Paul Stockton testified at the hearing. And reducing the number of clearances granted overall was also a recommendation of a Department of Defense committee and report on the Navy Yard incident.[13] The Office of Management and Budget made the recommendation in a February 2014 report to the president saying that "growth in the number of clearance-holders increases costs and exposes classified national security information, often at very sensitive levels, to an increasingly large population."[14]

Future analysis will undoubtedly make similar recommendations that both the number of secrets and the number of clearances be limited. But the question remains whether the personnel security clearance system, which has grown so big over the years, has the ability to contain itself. Given the tendency of bureaucracies to grow rather than shrink, I worry that the system does not possess the wherewithal to shrink itself. It needs help. Legislation can be one source of help in reducing the number of clearances. To mitigate the inability of the Executive Branch to contain growth in the number of secrets and clearances, some lawmakers have introduced legislation that would impose limits.[15] While these legislative efforts are not perfect (and have not been passed), it appears that attempts to limit the number of secrets and those with access to them are more likely to come from those with oversight responsibilities rather than from those within the system. Legislative proposals should be encouraged as a way to keep the conversation focused on the problem of too many people with clearances and too much classification overall.

Recommendation: Play by Your Own Rules

Security clearance professionals would do well to adhere to the policies they have developed for themselves. The example of fraudulent investigations is one illustration of how the government's specified policies all too often go unheeded. Another is in various administrations' stated policies protecting whistleblowers. For example, President-elect Obama promised new whistleblower protections during his administration. His transition website stated, "Often the best source of information about waste, fraud, and abuse in government is an existing government employee committed to public integrity and willing to speak out. Such acts of courage and patriotism, which can sometimes save lives and often save taxpayer dollars, should be encouraged rather than stifled." But he took that page down after the transition was complete.[16] According to Andy, the former Defense Department employee, the government stands to lose a lot when it retreats from its own intended purposes:

> And I . . . actually testified. . . . That, you know, the security clearance system is used as a punitive measure of management's tools, rather than on trying to determine reliability. When I testified, there was a specialist right next to me, an E4 Army type, also in uniform. We talked about the fact what when he discovered wrongdoing regarding the Abu Ghraib interrogations and reported it, they took his clearance. Are you kidding me? The guy reports something that he's supposed to and they revoke his clearance? This is where . . . leadership, the way they use [the security clearance system], completely makes a mockery of it, because it makes it a punitive tool rather than a bellwether of reliability for the purposes of having access to national security information.

Conclusion

This insiders' view of the personnel security clearance system has examined the process by which the federal government incorporates individuals into secret national security work. Through interviews with individuals who have experienced the system, I explored what happens when a system built to create and maintain a rational balance of secrecy turns irrational. I have also looked at how systems of security can inadvertently promote insecurity, and at how the state, through its treatment of some individuals in the personnel security clearance system, may be working against its own best interests. In doing so I have tried to illuminate the power relationship between individuals and the state through the voices of the system's participants.

Analyzing the processes by which individuals are inducted into national security jobs reveals that many facets of that process are flawed. Investigators are at times overworked, negligent, or dishonest.[17] Databases designed to "connect the dots" by monitoring and flagging risks are promised, but have yet to materialize. Methodologies to accurately assess and identify personality types that are predisposed to deceit or subterfuge are crude at best. The scientific basis for existing tools used in the process, like the polygraph, has been discredited. Random drug testing, while more scientifically sound, can also be inaccurate. But there is no rigorously scientific way to determine which federal workers are risks to the state. There are no diagnostic tools like the ones used in medical science to identify diseases. In many ways, however, it seems that is what those maintaining the personnel security clearance system are striving for.

One reason the system remains flawed is that, in the end, the clearance system processes people. Although developing a single process that will consistently and accurately evaluate and monitor every applicant's and employee's behavior and predilections is probably not feasible, the flaws in the existing system can lead to capriciousness. The system can be abused by those in power—those who retaliate against employees, such as whistleblowers—who in doing so embarrass the bureaucracy they serve.

The allegiance to the state of those who serve it is strong. But questions remain as to whether this allegiance is a fatal attraction. The loyalty demanded by the state is virtually blind. Most federal workers are resigned to follow the dictates of their responsibilities. But when they run afoul of the personnel security clearance system they are surprised by the punitive nature of the bureaucracy they encounter. I suggest, as others have suggested before me, that the punitive elements of the security clearance processes may be rooted in, among other historical and cultural origins, the Puritan ethic that was transplanted in the United States at its inception.[18]

Although I never lost a clearance, I did, over my twenty-three-year federal career, experience the power and weight of bureaucratic wrath. And it can be quite stressful. Once, while serving as spokesperson for a defense agency, I embarrassed my boss by confirming, for a journalist, certain facts in an annual counterintelligence publication that the agency had produced. Those "facts," although I did not know it at the time, were not true. My boss's response, "I want you out of your office by noon," was not an unusual bureaucratic reaction. But it left me quite anxious. I was removed from my office, moved to a smaller one, and told to find another job, which I did. During that time my boss also tried to demote me one full pay level. Fortunately another agency offered me a position before that happened.[19]

Such encounters always leave a residue of bitterness. I believe that the punitive nature of bureaucratic retaliation toward those who have sworn to defend it negatively impacts the very ethos the state needs to maintain it. By using such measures, it breaks with its own best tenets, codes of conduct, character, and spirit. By retaliating against workers, the state is working against itself.

Every year the U.S. Office of Personnel and Management conducts employee morale surveys of federal employees, noting that the way employees are treated is an important element in recruiting and maintaining talent. Even if we do not believe, as James Carroll does, that bureaucracy in the form of the national security state is "constitutionally hostile to human beings,"[20] we should care about recruiting talented people into government service.

As of the first quarter of 2015, according to a Pew Research Center analysis, more than one-third of the American labor force was between the ages of eighteen and thirty-four.[21] Experts are divided about what these "millennials" require in the workplace and from a career. Some have argued that the millennial generation is fundamentally different from the generations that came before them. They are more apt to demand that their work provide them with more than just good pay and security. Others argue that the generation is more like their predecessors than we think. Either way, some of these young people will venture into government service. Given the vast lifestyle choices for the new millennium, the question is, will they stay? Jill, though still a government supervisor, is now reluctant to recommend government service to young people after her husband lost his clearance, ". . . How do you even bring new people into that process when . . . it can destroy your life? . . . We're still living the victimization of what it cost us."

Clearance holders know that their allegiance is to the state. But what do they expect in return? A representative democracy should produce a strong state. And a strong state should guard its secrets.

But not at the needless expenditure of careers and the morale of those who serve it.

In the United States of America, "We the People" are the state. It is up to us to try to make a stronger nation, a more perfect union. To do so, we must remain mindful of "civil morals . . . those the citizen has toward the State and, conversely, those the State owes the individual."[22]

APPENDIX

Adjudicative Guidelines for Determining Eligibility
for Access to Classified Information

Code of Federal Regulations, Title 32—National Defense

Volume: 1
Date: 2012-07-01
Original Date: 2012-07-01
Title: Part 147—Adjudicative Guidelines for Determining Eligibility
for Access to Classified Information
Context: Title 32—National Defense. Subtitle A—Department of
Defense. Chapter I—Office of the Secretary of Defense. Subchapter D—Personnel, Military and Civilian.

Part 147—Adjudicative Guidelines for Determining Eligibility for Access to Classified Information

SUBPART A—ADJUDICATIVE GUIDELINES
Sec. 147.1: Introduction.
Sec. 147.2: Adjudicative process.
Sec. 147.3: Guideline A—Allegiance to the United States.
Sec. 147.4: Guideline B—Foreign influence.
Sec. 147.5: Guideline C—Foreign preference.
Sec. 147.6: Guideline D—Sexual behavior.
Sec. 147.7: Guideline E—Personal conduct.
Sec. 147.8: Guideline F—Financial considerations.
Sec. 147.9: Guideline G—Alcohol consumption.
Sec. 147.10: Guideline H—Drug involvement.
Sec. 147.11: Guideline I—Emotional, mental, and personality
disorders.

Authority:

E.O. 12968 (60 FR 40245, 3 CFR 1995 Comp., p 391).

Source:

63 FR 4573, Jan. 30, 1998, unless otherwise noted.

Subpart A—Adjudication

§ 147.1 Introduction.

The following adjudicative guidelines are established for all United States Government civilian and military personnel, consultants, contractors, employees of contractors, licensees, certificate holders or grantees and their employees and other individuals who require access to classified information. They apply to persons being considered for initial or continued eligibility for access to classified information, to include sensitive compartmented information and special access programs and are to be used by government departments and agencies in all final clearance determinations.

§ 147.2 Adjudicative process.

(a) The adjudicative process is an examination of a sufficient period of a person's life to make an affirmative determination that the person is eligible for a security clearance. Eligibility for access to classified information is predicated upon the individual meeting these personnel security guidelines. The adjudicative process is the careful weighing of a number of variables known as the whole person concept. Available, reliable information about the person, past and present, favorable and unfavorable, should be considered in reaching a determination. In evaluating the relevance of an individual's conduct, the adjudicator should consider the following actors:

(1) The nature, extent, and seriousness of the conduct;

(2) The circumstances surrounding the conduct, to include knowledgeable participation;

(3) The frequency and recency of the conduct;

(4) The individual's age and maturity at the time of the conduct;

(5) The voluntariness of participation;

(6) The presence or absence of rehabilitation and other pertinent behavioral changes;

(7) The motivation for the conduct;

(8) The potential for pressure, coercion, exploitation, or duress;

(9) The likelihood of continuation of recurrence.

(b) Each case must be judged on its own merits, and final determination remains the responsibility of the specific department or agency. Any doubt as to whether access to classified information is clearly consistent with national security will be resolved in favor of the national security.

(c) The ultimate determination of whether the granting or continuing of eligibility for a security clearance is clearly consistent with the interests of national security must be an overall common sense determination based upon careful consideration of the following, each of which is to be evaluated in the context of the whole person, as explained further below:

(1) Guideline A: Allegiance to the United States.

(2) Guideline B: Foreign influence.

(3) Guideline C: Foreign preference.

(4) Guideline D: Sexual behavior.

(5) Guideline E: Personal conduct.

(6) Guideline F: Financial considerations.

(7) Guideline G: Alcohol consumption.

(8) Guideline H: Drug involvement.

(9) Guideline I: Emotional, mental, and personality disorders.

(10) Guideline J: Criminal conduct.

(11) Guideline K: Security violations.

(12) Guideline L: Outside activities.

(13) Guideline M: Misuse of Information Technology Systems.

(d) Although adverse information concerning a single criterion may not be sufficient for an unfavorable determination, the individual may be disqualified if available information reflects a recent or recurring pattern of questionable judgment, irresponsibility, or emotionally unstable behavior. Notwithstanding, the whole person concept, pursuit of further investigations may be terminated by an appropriate adjudicative agency in the face of reliable, significant, disqualifying, adverse information.

(e) When information of security concern becomes known about an individual who is currently eligible for access to classified information, the adjudicator should consider whether the person:

(1) Voluntarily reported the information;

(2) Was truthful and complete in responding to questions;

(3) Sought assistance and followed professional guidance, where appropriate;

(4) Resolved or appears likely to favorably resolve the security concern;

(5) Has demonstrated positive changes in behavior and employment;

(6) Should have his or her access temporarily suspended pending final adjudication of the information.

(f) If after evaluating information of security concern, the adjudicator decides that the information is not serious enough to warrant a recommendation of disapproval or revocation of the security clearance, it may be appropriate to recommend approval with a warning that future incidents of a similar nature may result in revocation of access.

§ 147.3 Guideline A—Allegiance to the United States.

(a) *The concern.* An individual must be of unquestioned allegiance to the United States. The willingness to safeguard classified information is in doubt if there is any reason to suspect an individual's allegiance to the United States.

(b) *Conditions that could raise a security concern and may be disqualifying include:*

(1) Involvement in any act of sabotage, espionage, treason, terrorism, sedition, or other act whose aim is to overthrow the Government of the United States or alter the form of government by unconstitutional means;

(2) Association or sympathy with persons who are attempting to commit, or who are committing, any of the above acts;

(3) Association or sympathy with persons or organizations that advocate the overthrow of the United States Government, or any state or subdivision, by force or violence or by other unconstitutional means;

(4) Involvement in activities which unlawfully advocate or practice the commission of acts of force or violence to prevent others from exercising their rights under the Constitution or laws of the United States or of any state.

(c) *Conditions that could mitigate security concerns include:*

(1) The individual was unaware of the unlawful aims of the individual or organization and severed ties upon learning of these;

(2) The individual's involvement was only with the lawful or humanitarian aspects of such an organization;

(3) Involvement in the above activities occurred for only a short period of time and was attributable to curiosity or academic interest;

(4) The person has had no recent involvement or association with such activities.

§ 147.4 Guideline B—Foreign influence.

(a) *The concern.* A security risk may exist when an individual's immediate family, including cohabitants and other persons to whom he or she may be bound by affection, influence, or obligation are not citizens of the United States or may be subject to duress. These situations could create the potential for foreign influence that could result in the compromise of classified information. Contacts with citizens of other countries or financial interests in other countries are also relevant to security determinations if they make an individual potentially vulnerable to coercion, exploitation, or pressure.

(b) *Conditions that could raise a security concern and may be disqualifying include:*

(1) An immediate family member, or a person to whom the individual has close ties of affection or obligation, is a citizen of, or resident or present in, a foreign country;

(2) Sharing living quarters with a person or persons, regardless of their citizenship status, if the potential for adverse foreign influence or duress exists;

(3) Relatives, cohabitants, or associates who are connected with any foreign government;

(4) Failing to report, where required, associations with foreign nationals;

(5) Unauthorized association with a suspected or known collaborator or employee of a foreign intelligence service;

(6) Conduct which may make the individual vulnerable to coercion, exploitation, or pressure by a foreign government;

(7) Indications that representatives or nationals from a foreign country are acting to increase the vulnerability of the individual to possible future exploitation, coercion or pressure;

(8) A substantial financial interest in a country, or in any foreign owned or operated business that could make the individual vulnerable to foreign influence.

(c) *Conditions that could mitigate security concerns include:*

(1) A determination that the immediate family member(s) (spouse, father, mother, sons, daughters, brothers, sisters), cohabitant, or associate(s) in question are not agents of a foreign power or in a position to be exploited by a foreign power in a way that could force the individual to choose between loyalty to the person(s) involved and the United States;

(2) Contacts with foreign citizens are the result of official United States Government business;

(3) Contact and correspondence with foreign citizens are casual and infrequent;

(4) The individual has promptly complied with existing agency requirements regarding the reporting of contacts, requests, or threats from persons or organizations from a foreign country;

(5) Foreign financial interests are minimal and not sufficient to affect the individual's security responsibilities.

§ 147.5 Guideline C—Foreign preference.

(a) *The concern.* When an individual acts in such a way as to indicate a preference for a foreign country over the United States, then he or she may be prone to provide information or make decisions that are harmful to the interests of the United States.

(b) *Conditions that could raise a security concern and may be disqualifying include:*

(1) The exercise of dual citizenship;

(2) Possession and/or use of a foreign passport;

(3) Military service or a willingness to bear arms for a foreign country;

(4) Accepting educational, medical, or other benefits, such as retirement and social welfare, from a foreign country;

(5) Residence in a foreign country to meet citizenship requirements;

(6) Using foreign citizenship to protect financial or business interests in another country;

(7) Seeking or holding political office in the foreign country;

(8) Voting in foreign elections;

(9) Performing or attempting to perform duties, or otherwise acting, so as to serve the interests of another government in preference to the interests of the United States.

(c) *Conditions that could mitigate security concerns include:*

(1) Dual citizenship is based solely on parents' citizenship or birth in a foreign country;
(2) Indicators of possible foreign preference (e.g., foreign military service) occurred before obtaining United States citizenship;
(3) Activity is sanctioned by the United States;
(4) Individual has expressed a willingness to renounce dual citizenship.

§ 147.6 Guideline D—Sexual behavior.

(a) *The concern.* Sexual behavior is a security concern if it involves a criminal offense, indicates a personality or emotional disorder, may subject the individual to coercion, exploitation, or duress, or reflects lack of judgment or discretion.[1] Sexual orientation or preference may not be used as a basis for or a disqualifying factor in determining a person's eligibility for a security clearance.

(b) *Conditions that could raise a security concern and may be disqualifying include:*
(1) Sexual behavior of a criminal nature, whether or not the individual has been prosecuted;
(2) Compulsive or addictive sexual behavior when the person is unable to stop a pattern or self-destructive or high-risk behavior or that which is symptomatic of a personally disorder;
(3) Sexual behavior that causes an individual to be vulnerable to coercion, exploitation, or duress;
(4) Sexual behavior of a public nature and/or that which reflects lack of discretion or judgment.

(c) *Conditions that could mitigate security concerns include:*
(1) The behavior occurred during or prior to adolescence and there is no evidence of subsequent conduct of a similar nature;
(2) The behavior was not recent and there is no evidence of subsequent conduct of a similar nature;
(3) There is no other evidence of questionable judgment, irresponsibility, or emotional instability;
(4) The behavior no longer serves as a basis for coercion, exploitation, or duress.

1. The adjudicator should also consider guidelines pertaining to criminal conduct (Guideline J) and emotional, mental and personality disorders (Guideline I) in determining how to resolve the security concerns raised by sexual behavior.

§ 147.7 Guideline E—Personal conduct.

(a) *The concern.* Conduct involving questionable judgment, untrustworthiness, unreliability, lack of candor, dishonesty, or unwillingness to comply with rules and regulations could indicate that the person may not properly safeguard classified information. The following will normally result in an unfavorable clearance action or administrative termination of further processing for clearance eligibility:

    (1) Refusal to undergo or cooperate with required security processing, including medical and psychological testing;

    (2) Refusal to complete required security forms, releases, or provide full, frank and truthful answers to lawful questions of investigators, security officials or other representatives in connection with a personnel security or trustworthiness determination.

(b) *Conditions that could raise a security concern and may be disqualifying also include:*

    (1) Reliable, unfavorable information provided by associates, employers, coworkers, neighbors, and other acquaintances;

    (2) The deliberate omission, concealment, or falsification of relevant and material facts from any personnel security questionnaire, personal history statement, or similar form used to conduct investigations, determine employment qualifications, award benefits or status, determine security clearance eligibility or trustworthiness, or award fiduciary responsibilities;

    (3) Deliberately providing false or misleading information concerning relevant and material matters to an investigator, security official, competent medical authority, or other representative in connection with a personnel security or trustworthiness determination;

    (4) Personal conduct or concealment of information that may increase an individual's vulnerability to coercion, exploitation, or duties, such as engaging in activities which, if known, may affect the person's personal, professional, or community standing or render the person susceptible to blackmail;

    (5) A pattern of dishonesty or rule violations, including violation of any written or recorded agreement made between the individual and the agency;

    (6) Association with persons involved in criminal activity.

(c) *Conditions that could mitigate security concerns include:*

    (1) The information was unsubstantiated or not pertinent to a determination of judgment, trustworthiness, or reliability;

(2) The falsification was an isolated incident, was not recent, and the individual has subsequently provided correct information voluntarily;

(3) The individual made prompt, good faith efforts to correct the falsification before being confronted with the facts;

(4) Omission of material facts was caused or significantly contributed to by improper or inadequate advice of authorized personnel, and the previously omitted information was promptly and fully provided;

(5) The individual has taken positive steps to significantly reduce or eliminate vulnerability to coercion, exploitation, or duress;

(6) A refusal to cooperate was based on advice from legal counsel or other officials that the individual was not required to comply with security processing requirements and, upon being made aware of the requirement, fully and truthfully provided the requested information;

(7) Association with persons involved in criminal activities has ceased.

§ 147.8   Guideline F—Financial considerations.

(a) *The concern.* An individual who is financially overextended is at risk of having to engage in illegal acts to generate funds. Unexplained affluence is often linked to proceeds from financially profitable criminal acts.

(b) *Conditions that could raise a security concern and may be disqualifying include*:

(1) A history of not meeting financial obligations;

(2) Deceptive or illegal financial practices such as embezzlement, employee theft, check fraud, income tax evasion, expense account fraud, filing deceptive loan statements, and other intentional financial breaches of trust;

(3) Inability or unwillingness to satisfy debts;

(4) Unexplained affluence;

(5) Financial problems that are linked to gambling, drug abuse, alcoholism, or other issues of security concern.

(c) *Conditions that could mitigate security concerns include:*

(1) The behavior was not recent;

(2) It was an isolated incident;

(3) The conditions that resulted in the behavior were largely beyond the person's control (e.g., loss of employment, a business

downturn, unexpected medical emergency, or a death, divorce or separation);

(4) The person has received or is receiving counseling for the problem and there are clear indications that the problem is being resolved or is under control;

(5) The affluence resulted from a legal source;

(6) The individual initiated a good-faith effort to repay overdue creditors or otherwise resolve debts.

§ 147.9 Guideline G—Alcohol consumption.

(a) *The concern.* Excessive alcohol consumption often leads to the exercise of questionable judgment, unreliability, failure to control impulses, and increases the risk of unauthorized disclosure of classified information due to carelessness.

(b) *Conditions that could raise a security concern and may be disqualifying include:*

(1) Alcohol-related incidents away from work, such as driving while under the influence, fighting, child or spouse abuse, or other criminal incidents related to alcohol use;

(2) Alcohol-related incidents at work, such as reporting for work or duty in an intoxicated or impaired condition, or drinking on the job;

(3) Diagnosis by a credentialed medical professional (e.g., physician, clinical psychologist, or psychiatrist) of alcohol abuse or alcohol dependence;

(4) Evaluation of alcohol abuse or alcohol dependence by a licensed clinical social worker who is a staff member of a recognized alcohol treatment program;

(5) Habitual or binge consumption of alcohol to the point of impaired judgment;

(6) Consumption of alcohol, subsequent to a diagnosis of alcoholism by a credentialed medical professional and following completion of an alcohol rehabilitation program.

(c) *Conditions that could mitigate security concerns include:*

(1) The alcohol related incidents do not indicate a pattern;

(2) The problem occurred a number of years ago and there is no indication of a recent problem;

(3) Positive changes in behavior supportive of sobriety;

(4) Following diagnosis of alcohol abuse or alcohol dependence, the individual has successfully completed inpatient or outpatient

rehabilitation along with aftercare requirements, participates frequently in meetings of Alcoholics Anonymous or a similar organization, has abstained from alcohol for a period of at least 12 months, and received a favorable prognosis by a credentialed medical professional or a licensed clinical social worker who is a staff member of a recognized alcohol treatment program.

§ 147.10   Guideline H—Drug involvement.

(a) *The concern.*

    (1) Improper or illegal involvement with drugs raises questions regarding an individual's willingness or ability to protect classified information. Drug abuse or dependence may impair social or occupational functioning, increasing the risk of an unauthorized disclosure of classified information.

    (2) Drugs are defined as mood and behavior altering substances, and include:

        (i) Drugs, materials, and other chemical compounds identified and listed in the Controlled Substances Act of 1970, as amended (e.g., marijuana or cannabis, depressants, narcotics, stimulants, and hallucinogens),

        (ii) Inhalants and other similar substances.

    (3) Drug abuse is the illegal use of a drug or use of a legal drug in a manner that deviates from approved medical direction.

(b) *Conditions that could raise a security concern and may be disqualifying include:*

    (1) Any drug abuse (see above definition);

    (2) Illegal drug possession, including cultivation, processing, manufacture, purchase, sale, or distribution;

    (3) Diagnosis by a credentialed medical professional (e.g., physician, clinical psychologist, or psychiatrist) of drug abuse or drug dependence;

    (4) Evaluation of drug abuse or drug dependence by a licensed clinical social worker who is a staff member of a recognized drug treatment program;

    (5) Failure to successfully complete a drug treatment program prescribed by a credentialed medical professional. Recent drug involvement, especially following the granting of a security clearance, or an expressed intent not to discontinue use, will almost invariably result in an unfavorable determination.

(c) *Conditions that could mitigate security concerns include:*
  (1) The drug involvement was not recent;
  (2) The drug involvement was an isolated or aberration event;
  (3) A demonstrated intent not to abuse any drugs in the future;
  (4) Satisfactory completion of a prescribed drug treatment program, including rehabilitation and aftercare requirements, without recurrence of abuse, and a favorable prognosis by a credentialed medical professional.

§ 147.11 Guideline I—Emotional, mental, and personality disorders.

(a) *The concern:* Emotional, mental, and personality disorders can cause a significant deficit in an individual's psychological, social and occupation functioning. These disorders are of security concern because they may indicate a defect in judgment, reliability, or stability. A credentialed mental health professional (e.g., clinical psychologist or psychiatrist), employed by, acceptable to or approved by the government, should be utilized in evaluating potentially disqualifying and mitigating information fully and properly, and particularly for consultation with the individual's mental health care provider.

(b) *Conditions that could raise a security concern and may be disqualifying include:*
  (1) An opinion by a credentialed mental health professional that the individual has a condition or treatment that may indicate a defect in judgment, reliability, or stability;
  (2) Information that suggests that an individual has failed to follow appropriate medical advice relating to treatment of a condition, e.g., failure to take prescribed medication;
  (3) A pattern of high-risk, irresponsible, aggressive, anti-social or emotionally unstable behavior;
  (4) Information that suggests that the individual's current behavior indicates a defect in his or her judgment or reliability.

(c) *Conditions that could mitigate security concerns include:*
  (1) There is no indication of a current problem;
  (2) Recent opinion by a credentialed mental health professional that an individual's previous emotional, mental, or personality disorder is cured, under control or in remission and has a low probability of recurrence or exacerbation;

(3) The past emotional instability was a temporary condition (e.g., one caused by a death, illness, or marital breakup), the situation has been resolved, and the individual is no longer emotionally unstable.

§ 147.12 Guideline J—Criminal conduct.

(a) *The concern.* A history or pattern of criminal activity creates doubt about a person's judgment, reliability, and trustworthiness.

(b) *Conditions that could raise a security concern and may be disqualifying include:*
  (1) Allegations or admissions of criminal conduct, regardless of whether the person was formally charged;
  (2) A single serious crime or multiple lesser offenses.

(c) *Conditions that could mitigate security concerns include:*
  (1) The criminal behavior was not recent;
  (2) The crime was an isolated incident;
  (3) The person was pressured or coerced into committing the act and those pressures are no longer present in that person's life;
  (4) The person did not voluntarily commit the act and/or the factors leading to the violation are not likely to recur;
  (5) Acquittal;
  (6) There is clear evidence of successful rehabilitation.

§ 147.13 Guideline K—Security violations.

(a) *The concern.* Noncompliance with security regulations raises doubt about an individual's trustworthiness, willingness, and ability to safeguard classified information.

(b) *Conditions that could raise a security concern and may be disqualifying include:*
  (1) Unauthorized disclosure of classified information;
  (2) Violations that are deliberate or multiple or due to negligence.

(c) *Conditions that could mitigate security concerns include actions that:*
  (1) Were inadvertent;
  (2) Were isolated or infrequent;
  (3) Were due to improper or inadequate training;
  (4) Demonstrate a positive attitude towards the discharge of security responsibilities.

§ 147.14 Guideline L—Outside activities.

(a) *The concern.* Involvement in certain types of outside employment or activities is of security concern if it poses a conflict with an individual's security responsibilities and could create an increased risk of unauthorized disclosure of classified information.

(b) *Conditions that could raise a security concern and may be disqualifying include any service, whether compensated, volunteer, or employment with:*

   (1) A foreign country;

   (2) Any foreign national;

   (3) A representative of any foreign interest;

   (4) Any foreign, domestic, or international organization or person engaged in analysis, discussion, or publication of material on intelligence, defense, foreign affairs, or protected technology.

(c) *Conditions that could mitigate security concerns include:*

   (1) Evaluation of the outside employment or activity indicates that it does not pose a conflict with an individual's security responsibilities;

   (2) The individual terminates the employment or discontinues the activity upon being notified that it is in conflict with his or her security responsibilities.

§ 147.15 Guideline M—Misuse of Information technology systems.

(a) *The concern.* Noncompliance with rules, procedures, guidelines, or regulations pertaining to information technology systems may raise security concerns about an individual's trustworthiness, willingness, and ability to properly protect classified systems, networks, and information. Information Technology Systems include all related equipment used for the communication, transmission, processing, manipulation, and storage of classified or sensitive information.

(b) *Conditions that could raise a security concern and may be disqualifying include:*

   (1) Illegal or unauthorized entry into any information technology system;

   (2) Illegal or unauthorized modification, destruction, manipulation or denial of access to information residing on an information technology system;

(3) Removal (or use) of hardware, software, or media from any information technology system without authorization, when specifically prohibited by rules, procedures, guidelines or regulations;

(4) Introduction of hardware, software, or media into any information technology system without authorization, when specifically prohibited by rules, procedures, guidelines or regulations.

(c) *Conditions that could mitigate security concerns include:*

(1) The misuse was not recent or significant;

(2) The conduct was unintentional or inadvertent;

(3) The introduction or removal of media was authorized;

(4) The misuse was an isolated event;

(5) The misuse was followed by a prompt, good faith effort to correct the situation.

Subpart B—Investigative Standards

§ 147.18   Introduction.

The following investigative standards are established for all United States Government civilian and military personnel, consultants, contractors, employees of contractors, licensees, certificate holders or grantees and their employees and other individuals who require access to classified information, to include Sensitive Compartmented Information and Special Access Programs, and are to be used by government departments and agencies as the investigative basis for final clearance determinations. However, nothing in these standards prohibits an agency from using any lawful investigative procedures in addition to these requirements in order to resolve any issue identified in the course of a background investigation or reinvestigation.

§ 147.19   The three standards.

There are three standards (Attachment D to this subpart part summarizes when to use each one):

(a) The investigation and reinvestigation standards for "L" access authorizations and for access to confidential and secret (including all secret-level Special Access Programs not specifically approved for enhanced investigative requirements by an official authorized to establish Special Access Programs by section in 4.4 of Executive Order 12958) (60 FR 19825, 3 CFR 1995 Comp., p. 33);

(b)   The investigation standard for "Q" access authorizations and for access to top secret (including top secret Special Access Programs) and Sensitive Compartmented Information;

(c)   The reinvestigation standard for continued access to the levels listed in paragraph (b) of this section.

§ 147.20   Exception to periods of coverage.

Some elements of standards specify a period of coverage (e.g., seven years). Where appropriate, such coverage may be shortened to the period from the subject's eighteenth birthday to the present or to two years, whichever is longer.

§ 147.21   Expanding investigations.

Investigations and reinvestigations may be expanded under the provisions of Executive Order 12968 (60 FR 40245, 3 CFR 1995 Comp., p. 391) and other applicable statutes and Executive Orders.

§ 147.22   Transferability.

Investigations that satisfy the requirements of a given standard and are current meet the investigative requirements for all levels specified for the standard. They shall be mutually and reciprocally accepted by all agencies.

§ 147.23   Breaks in service.

If a person who requires access has been retired or separated from U.S. government employment for less than two years and is the subject of an investigation that is otherwise current, the agency regranting the access will, as a minimum, review an updated Standard Form 86 and applicable records. A reinvestigation is not required unless the review indicates the person may no longer satisfy the standards of Executive Order 12968 (60 FR 40245, 3 CFR 1995 Comp., p. 391); (Attachment D to this subpart, Table 2).

§ 147.24   The national agency check.

The National Agency Check is a part of all investigations and reinvestigations. It consists of a review of;

(a)   Investigative and criminal history files of the FBI, including a technical fingerprint search;

(b)   OPM's Security/Suitability Investigations Index;

(c)   DoD's Defense Clearance and Investigations Index;

(d)   Such other national agencies (e.g., CIA, INS) as appropriate to the individual's background.

Pt. 147, Subpt. B, Att. A: Attachment A to Subpart B of Part 147—Standard A—National Agency Check With Local Agency Checks and Credit Check (NACLC)

(a)   *Applicability.* Standard A applies to investigations and reinvestigations for;

    (1)   Access to CONFIDENTIAL and SECRET (including all SECRET-level Special Access Programs not specifically approved for enhanced investigative requirements by an official authorized to establish Special Access Programs by sect. 4.4 of Executive Order 12958) (60 FR 19825, 3 CFR 1995 Comp., p. 333);

    (2)   "L" access authorizations.

(b)   *For Reinvestigation: When to Reinvestigate.* The reinvestigation may be initiated at any time following completion of, but not later than ten years (fifteen years for CONFIDENTIAL) from the date of, the previous investigation or reinvestigation. (Attachment D to this subpart, Table 2, reflects the specific requirements for when to request a reinvestigation, including when there has been a break in service.)

(c)   *Investigative Requirements.* Investigative requirements are as follows:

    (1)   *Completion of Forms:* Completion of Standard Form 86, including applicable releases and supporting documentation.

    (2)   *National Agency Check:* Completion of a National Agency Check.

    (3)   *Financial Review:* Verification of the subject's financial status, including credit bureau checks covering all locations where the subject has resided, been employed, or attended school for six months or more for the past seven years.

    (4)   *Date and Place of Birth:* Corroboration of date and place of birth through a check of appropriate documentation, if not completed in any previous investigation; a check of Bureau of Vital Statistics records when any discrepancy is found to exist.

    (5)   *Local Agency Checks:* As a minimum, all investigations will include checks of law enforcement agencies having jurisdiction where the subject has lived, worked, and/or attended school within the last five years, and, if applicable, of the appropriate agency for any identified arrests.

(d) *Expanding the Investigation:* The investigation may be expanded if necessary to determine if access is clearly consistent with the national security.

Pt. 147, Subpt. B, Att. B: Attachment B to Subpart B of Part 147—Standard B—Single Scope Background Investigation (SSBI)

(a) *Applicability.* Standard B applies to initial investigations for;
   (1) Access to TOP SECRET (including TOP SECRET Special Access Programs) and Sensitive Compartment Information;
   (2) "Q" access authorizations.
(b) *Investigative Requirements.* Investigative requirements are as follows:
   (1) *Completion of Forms:* Completion of Standard Form 86, including applicable releases and supporting documentation.
   (2) *National Agency Check:* Completion of a National Agency Check.
   (3) *National Agency Check for the Spouse or Cohabitant (if applicable):* Completion of a National Agency Check, without fingerprint cards, for the spouse or cohabitant.
   (4) *Date and Place of Birth:* Corroboration of date and place of birth through a check of appropriate documentation; a check of Bureau of Vital Statistics records when any discrepancy is found to exist.
   (5) *Citizenship:* For individuals born outside the United States, verification of US citizenship directly from the appropriate registration authority; verification of US citizenship or legal status of foreign-born immediate family members (spouse, cohabitant, father, mother, sons, daughters, brothers, sisters).
   (6) *Education:* Corroboration of most recent or most significant claimed attendance, degree, or diploma. Interviews of appropriate educational sources if education is a primary activity of the subject during the most recent three years.
   (7) *Employment:* Verification of all employments for the past seven years; personal interviews of sources (supervisors, coworkers, or both) for each employment of six months or more; corroboration through records or sources of all periods of unemployment exceeding sixty days; verification of all prior federal and military service, including discharge type. For military members, all service within one branch of the armed forces will be considered as one employment, regardless of assignments.

(8) *References:* Four references, of whom at least two are developed; to the extent practicable, all should have social knowledge of the subject and collectively span at least the last seven years.

(9) *Former Spouse:* An interview of any former spouse divorced within the last ten years.

(10) *Neighborhoods:* Confirmation of all residences for the last three years through appropriate interviews with neighbors and through records reviews.

(11) *Financial Review:* Verification of the subject's financial status, including credit bureau checks covering all locations where subject has resided, been employed, and/or attended school for six months or more for the last seven years.

(12) *Local Agency Checks:* A check of appropriate criminal history records covering all locations where, for the last ten years, the subject has resided, been employed, and/or attended school for six months or more, including current residence regardless of duration. *Note:* If no residence, employment, or education exceeds six months, local agency checks should be performed as deemed appropriate.

(13) *Public Records:* Verification of divorces, bankruptcies, and other court actions, whether civil or criminal, involving the subject.

(14) *Subject Interview:* A subject interview, conducted by trained security, investigative, or counterintelligence personnel. During the investigation, additional subject interviews may be conducted to collect relevant information, to resolve significant inconsistencies, or both. Sworn statements and unsworn declarations may be taken whenever appropriate.

(15) *Polygraph (only in agencies with approved personnel security polygraph programs):* In departments or agencies with policies sanctioning the use of the polygraph for personnel security purposes, the investigation may include a polygraph examination, conducted by a qualified polygraph examiner.

(c) *Expanding the Investigation.* The investigation may be expanded as necessary. As appropriate, interviews with anyone able to provide information or to resolve issues, including but not limited to cohabitants, relatives, psychiatrists, psychologists, other medical professionals, and law enforcement professionals may be conducted.

Pt. 147, Subpt. B, Att. C: Attachment C to Subpart B of Part 147—
Standard C—Single Scope Background Investigation Periodic
Reinvestigation (SSBI-PR)

(a) *Applicability.* Standard C applies to reinvestigation for;
   (1) *Access to* TOP SECRET *(including* TOP SECRET *Special Access Programs) and Sensitive Compartmented Information;*
   (2) "Q" access authorizations.
(b) *When to Reinvestigate.* The reinvestigation may be initiated at any time following completion of, but not later than five years from the date of, the previous investigation (see Attachment D to this subpart, Table 2).
(c) *Reinvestigative Requirements.* Reinvestigative requirements are as follows:
   (1) *Completion of Forms:* Completion of Standard Form 86, including applicable releases and supporting documentation.
   (2) *National Agency Check:* Completion of a National Agency Check (fingerprint cards are required only if there has not been a previous valid technical check of the FBI).
   (3) *National Agency Check for the Spouse or Cohabitant (if applicable):* Completion of a National Agency Check, without fingerprint cards, for the spouse or cohabitant. The National Agency Check for the spouse or cohabitant is not required if already completed in conjunction with a previous investigation or reinvestigation.
   (4) *Employment:* Verification of all employments since the last investigation. Attempts to interview a sufficient number of sources (supervisors, coworkers, or both) at all employments of six months or more. For military members, all services within one branch of the armed forces will be considered as one employment, regardless of assignments.
   (5) *References:* Interviews with two character references who are knowledgeable of the subject; at least one will be a developed reference. To the extent practical, both should have social knowledge of the subject and collectively span the entire period of the reinvestigation. As appropriate, additional interviews may be conducted, including with cohabitants and relatives.
   (6) *Neighborhoods:* Interviews of two neighbors in the vicinity of the subject's most recent residence of six months or more. Confirmation of current residence regardless of length.

(7) *Financial Review—Financial Status:* Verification of the subject's financial status, including credit bureau checks covering all locations where subject has resided, been employed, and/or attended school for six months or more for the period covered by the reinvestigation;

    (ii) *Check of Treasury's Financial Data Base:* Agencies may request the Department of the Treasury, under terms and conditions prescribed by the Secretary of the Treasury, to search automated data bases consisting of reports of currency transactions by financial institutions, international transportation of currency or monetary instruments, foreign bank and financial accounts, and transactions under $10,000 that are reported as possible money laundering violations.

(8) *Local Agency Checks:* A check of appropriate criminal history records covering all locations where, during the period covered by the reinvestigation, the subject has resided, been employed, and/or attended school for six months or more, including current residence regardless of duration. (Note: If no residence, employment, or education exceeds six months, local agency checks should be performed as deemed appropriate.)

(9) *Former Spouse:* An interview with any former spouse unless the divorce took place before the date of the last investigation or reinvestigation.

(10) *Public Records:* Verification of divorces, bankruptcies, and other court actions, whether civil or criminal, involving the subject since the date of the last investigation.

(11) *Subject Interview:* A subject interview, conducted by trained security, investigative, or counterintelligence personnel. During the reinvestigation, additional subject interviews may be conducted to collect relevant information, to resolve significant inconsistencies, or both. Sworn statements and unsworn declarations may be taken whenever appropriate.

(d) *Expanding the Reinvestigation:* The reinvestigation may be expanded as necessary. As appropriate, interviews with anyone able to provide information or to resolve issues, including but not limited to cohabitants, relatives, psychiatrists, psychologists, other medical professionals, and law enforcement professionals may be conducted.

Pt. 147, Subpt. B, Att. D: Attachment D to Subpart B of Part 147—Decision Tables

Table 1. Which investigation to request

IF THE REQUIREMENT IS FOR	AND THE PERSON HAS THIS ACCESS	BASED ON THIS INVESTIGATION	THEN THE INVESTIGATION REQUIRED IS	USING STANDARD
Confidential Secret; "L"	None	None	NACLC	A
		Out of date NACLC or SSBI		
	Conf. Sec.; "L"			
Top Secret, SCI; "Q"	None	None	SSBI	B
	None; Conf. Sec.; "L"	Current or out of date NACLC		
		Out of date SSBI		
	TS, SCI; "Q"		SSBI-PR	C

Table 2. Reinvestigation requirements

IF THE REQUIREMENT IS FOR	AND THE AGE OF THE INVESTIGATION IS	TYPE REQUIRED IF THERE HAS BEEN A BREAK IN SERVICE OF	
		0–23 MONTHS	24 MONTHS OR MORE
Confidential	0–14 yrs., 11 mos.	None*	NACLC
	15 yrs. or more	NACLC	
Secret; "L"	0–9 yrs., 11 mos.	None*	
	10 yrs. or more	NACLC	
Top Secret, SCI; "Q"	0–4 yrs., 11 mos.	None*	SSBI
	5 yrs. or more	SSBI-PR	

* As a minimum, review an updated Standard Form 84 and applicable records. A reinvestigation (NACLC or SSBI-PR) is not required unless the review indicates the person may no longer satisfy the standards of Executive Order 12968.

Subpart C—Guidelines for Temporary Access

§ 147.28 Introduction.

The following minimum investigative standards, implementing section 3.3 of Executive Order 12968, *Access to Classified Information,* are established for all United States Government and military personnel, consultants, contractors, subcontractors, employees of contractors, licensees, certificate holders or grantees and their employees and other individuals who require access to classified information before the appropriate investigation can be completed and a final determination made.

§ 147.29 Temporary eligibility for access.

Based on a justified need meeting the requirements of section 3.3 of Executive Order 12968, temporary eligibility for access may be granted before investigations are complete and favorably adjudicated, where official functions must be performed prior to completion of the investigation and adjudication process. The temporary eligibility will be valid until completion of the investigation and adjudication; however, the agency granting it may revoke it at any time based on unfavorable information identified in the course of the investigation.

§ 147.30 Temporary eligibility for access at the confidential and secret levels and temporary eligibility for "L" access authorization.

As a minimum, such temporary eligibility requires completion of the Standard Form 86, including any applicable supporting documentation, favorable review of the form by the appropriate adjudicating authority, and submission of a request for an expedited National Agency Check with Local Agency Checks and Credit (NACLC).

§ 147.31 Temporary eligibility for access at the top secret levels and temporary eligibility for "Q" access authorization: For someone who is the subject of a favorable investigation not meeting the investigative standards for access at those levels.

As a minimum, such temporary eligibility requires completion of the Standard Form 86, including any applicable supporting documentation, favorable review of the form by the appropriate adjudicating authority, and expedited submission of a request for a Single Scope Background Investigation (SSBI).

§ 147.32   Temporary eligibility for access at the top secret and sci levels and temporary eligibility for "Q" access authorization: For someone who is not the subject of a current, favorable personnel or personnel-security investigation of any kind.

As a minimum, such temporary eligibility requires completion of the Standard Form 86, including any applicable supporting documentation, favorable review of the form by the appropriate adjudicating authority, immediate submission of a request for an expedited Single Scope Background Investigation (SSBI), and completion and favorable review by the appropriate adjudicating authority of relevant criminal history and investigative records of the Federal Bureau of Investigation and of information in the Security/Suitability Investigations Index (SII) and the Defense Clearance and Investigations Index (DCII).

§ 147.33   Additional requirements by agencies.

Temporary eligibility for access must satisfy these minimum investigative standards, but agency heads may establish additional requirements based on the sensitivity of the particular, identified categories of classified information necessary to perform the lawful and authorized functions that are the basis for granting temporary eligibility for access. However, no additional requirements shall exceed the common standards for background investigations developed under section 3.2(b) of Executive Order 12968. Temporary eligibility for access is valid only at the agency granting it and at other agencies who expressly agree to accept it and acknowledge understanding of its investigative basis. It is further subject to limitations specified in sections 2.4(d) and 3.3 of Executive Order 12968, *Access to Classified Information*.

NOTES

1. Blacklists were compiled by the House Committee on Un-American Activities and the Senate Committee led by Senator Joseph McCarthy during the Communist hysteria of the 1950s. The personnel clearance policies, methodologies, and regulations established during that singularly paranoid era in the United States (up until the more recent one ushered in by the attacks of September 11, 2001) continue to imbue the process today.

2. Nathaniel Hawthorne's 1850 novel explores themes of legalism, sin, and guilt. It is notable that many of these same themes were taken up a century later in *The Crucible*, Arthur Miller's 1953 play about the Salem witch trials, which was written as an allegory of McCarthyism. These themes are also explored in what Max Weber referenced as the "Protestant Ethic" underlying the modern capitalist state. In *The Protestant Ethic and the Spirit of Capitalism*, Weber wrote that capitalism evolved when the Protestant (particularly Calvinist) ethic influenced large numbers of people to engage in work in the secular world, accumulating wealth for investment.

3. Fiction can sometimes best describe reality. Franz Kafka's 1925 novel *The Trial* tells the story of a man arrested and prosecuted without the nature of his crime being revealed to him. Authors provide insights into societal truths through art. Such truths may not always be personal. But sometimes they are. Hawthorne may not have been an adulterer. And Miller did not hold a security clearance. But he was questioned by the House Committee on Un-American Activities in 1956 and convicted of "contempt of Congress" for refusing to identify others present at meetings he had attended (Loftus, "Miller Convicted").

1. THE MANY FACES OF A THREAT

1. First Amendment Center, "Benjamin Bache and the Fight for a Free Press." www.firstamendmentcenter.org.
2. Bird and Sherwin, *American Prometheus*, 464.
3. Bird and Sherwin, *American Prometheus*, 465.
4. The Rosenbergs were tried under the Espionage Act of 1917, passed by President Wilson.
5. Sartre, "Mad Beasts," 207–11.
6. For more on Hollywood blacklists, see Gladchuck, *Hollywood and Anticommunism*, and Bernstein, *Inside Out*.
7. Simpson and McDaniel, "Prologue."
8. Johnson, *The Lavender Scare*, 166.
9. Johnson, *The Lavender Scare*, 168.
10. *Employment of Homosexuals and Other Sex Perverts in Government* (1950). This was also known as the Hoey Report or Hoey Investigation.
11. Bérubé, *Coming Out under Fire*.
12. One of the individuals I interviewed explained that the results of such reports were "buried" because the commonly held belief was that "homosexuals could be blackmailed."
13. Allen, "Mission Diversify."
14. Panetta, speech to Defense Department employees.
15. Yenne, *Rising Sons*.
16. U.S. Merit Systems Protection Board, *Managing Public Employees*.
17. Harnden, "The Spies Who Loved."
18. Pressly, "The Spy Who Loved Her."
19. U.S. Department of Justice, *A Review of FBI Security Programs*.
20. U.S. Department of Defense PERSEREC, "Hanssen."
21. Weiner, "Why I Spied."
22. Apple, "25 Years Later."
23. Specifically, the papers revealed that the United States had secretly enlarged the scale of the Vietnam War with the bombings of nearby Cambodia and Laos which were not reported in the mainstream media.
24. On June 2, 2015, the U.S. Senate passed, and President Obama signed, the USA Freedom Act, which modified provisions of the USA Patriot Act (2001) and imposed some legal limits on the bulk collection of telecommunications data on U.S. citizens by American intelligence agencies. The new restrictions were seen by many as resulting from Snowden's revelations.
25. Marcus, "The Insufferable Snowden."
26. Grand, "Edward Snowden."

27. Schmitt, "C.I.A. Warning on Snowden."
28. Popkin, "Ana Montes."
29. Frieden, "Ex-State Official, Wife Accused of Spying for Cuba."
30. Gillum and Tucker, "How Can Red Flags Be Missed?"
31. U.S. Department of Defense PERSEREC, "Hanssen."
32. Assigned in 2009 to an Army unit in Iraq, Manning had access to classified databases. In early 2010 she leaked classified information and confided this to Adrian Lamo, an online acquaintance. Lamo informed Army Counterintelligence, and Manning was arrested in May that same year. The material included videos of the July 12, 2007, Baghdad airstrike, and the 2009 Granai airstrike in Afghanistan. Much of the material was published by WikiLeaks or its media partners between April and November 2010 (Poulsen and Zetter, "U.S. Intelligence Analyst Arrested").
33. Zetter, "Security Jolt in WikiLeaks Case."
34. Clark, "Pentagon's Key Whistle Blower Counselor Moves."
35. *Federal Soup*, "Directive Extends Whistleblower Protections."
36. Taylor and Landay, "Obama's Crackdown."
37. Sledge, "Unhappy with U.S. Foreign Policy?"
38. McHugh, *Army Directive 2013-18*.
39. Greenwald, "On the Espionage Act Charges."
40. Currier, "Charting Obama's Crackdown."

2. THE PERSONNEL SECURITY CLEARANCE PROCESS

1. There is some uncertainty about who coined the phrase originally. It could have been Alan Barth, writing for the *New Republic* in 1943, or it might have been *Washington Post* chairman and CEO Philip Graham (Shafer, "Who Said It First?"). Schafer thinks it was Barth, although Graham tends to get the credit.
2. My father also points to the importance of choosing credible journalists as one's research assistants, noting that "Some conform to the highest journalistic standards; others to the lowest. This is, unfortunately, also true of universities" (Deutscher, *Accommodating Diversity*, 70).
3. The term "need to know," when used by the government describes the restriction of data that are considered sensitive. Under need-to-know restrictions, even if one has all the necessary official approvals (such as a security clearance) to gain access to certain information, one would not be given access to information, unless one has a specific need to know. Access to the information must be necessary for the conduct of one's official duties.

4. Executive Order 12968.
5. U.S. Department of State, "All about Security Clearances."
6. LaFlure, "Security Clearance Lapses."
7. IRTPA addresses many different facets of information gathering and the intelligence community. IRTPA's eight titles reflect its broad scope, which in addition to Security Clearances includes: Reform of the Intelligence Community; Federal Bureau of Investigation; Transportation Security; Border Protection, Immigration, and Visa Matters; Terrorism Prevention; Implementation of 9/11 Commission Recommendations; and a requirement that the Department of Homeland Security ensure that "the civil rights and civil liberties of persons are not diminished by efforts, activities, and programs aimed at securing the homeland" (Intelligence Reform and Terrorism Prevention Act).
8. Wise, "Contractor Responsible."
9. Forensic Toxicology Drug Testing Laboratory at Fort George G. Meade Maryland, "The History of Drug Testing."
10. Rhem, "Who's Doing What."
11. U.S. Department of Defense, Office of Inspector General, "Frequently Asked Questions."
12. U.S. Department of Labor, Office of the Assistant Secretary for Policy, "elaws."
13. According to the Navy Drug Screening Laboratory, "each specimen bottle is assigned a unique Laboratory Accession Number (LAN). The LAN for each specimen is placed on the chain-of-custody document, and a label imprinted with the LAN is affixed to each bottle. Each specimen is retained in the accessioning area until it is approved for disposal" (Navy Drug Screening Laboratory San Diego, "Frequently Asked Questions").
14. Tully, "Know the Right Thing."
15. Emergency brand Detox Pills claim to allow you to pass a toxin-free urine sample drug test for almost any substance. "Rapid Clear Emergency Capsules are laboratory designed for the perfect detoxification solution. Our Emergency Detox Capsules become effective in as little as 45 minutes" (Rapid Clear).
16. Tully, "Know the Right Thing."
17. Polygraph Investigative Services, "FAQs."
18. Telephone conversation between the author and a researcher employed at the Department of Defense National Center for Credibility Assessment, September 12, 2013.
19. Polygraph Investigative Services, "FAQs."

20. Becker, "Doubts about Polygraphs."
21. Taylor, "As Polygraph Screening Flourishes."
22. Taylor, "Sen. Charles Grassley Seeks Probe."
23. Howard, "What Federal Applicants Should Know."
24. National Center for Credibility Assessment, "PDD Program." According to its website, the PDD Program is an academically challenging 520-hour series of courses that prepares the student to begin a polygraph career in law enforcement or counterintelligence.
25. Howard, "What Federal Applicants Should Know."
26. Employee Polygraph Protection (EPP), 29 U.S. Code, chapter 22.
27. Taylor, "Sen. Charles Grassley Seeks Probe."
28. National Center for Credibility Assessment, "PDD Program."
29. Stein, "Lie Detectors Lie."
30. National Research Council, *The Polygraph and Lie Detection*, 170.
31. *Federal Soup*, "Failed FBI Polygraph," The Federal Soup website (FederalSoup.com) is designed as a resource for federal employees about their career, pay, benefits, financial planning, and retirement options and is also the portal to weekly issues of the *Federal Employees News Digest*, benefits guides, and the annual *Federal Employees Almanac*.
32. Taylor, "FBI Turns Away Many Applicants."
33. Taylor, "FBI Turns Away Many Applicants."
34. Stein, "Lie Detectors Lie."
35. National Center for Credibility Assessment, "PDD Program." Indeed, even before the Obama administration's emphasis on insider threats, the now-defunct Department of Defense Counterintelligence Field Activity published an entire manual under the authority of DoD Directive 5210.48, DoD Polygraph Program, the purpose of which was to "prescribe uniform Psychophysiological Detection of Deception (PDDI polygraph) procedures" (U.S. Department of Defense, Counterintelligence Field Activity, *Federal Psychophysiol Detection*).
36. Joint Security and Suitability Reform Team, "Security and Suitability Process Reform."
37. U.S. Department of Defense, Defense Security Service, "Joint Personnel Adjudication System (JPAS)."
38. U.S. Department of Defense, Personnel and Security Research Center, "Initiatives."
39. Code of Federal Regulations, Title 32.
40. U.S. Department of Defense, Defense Security Service, "Electronic Fingerprint Capture Options."

41. U.S. Department of Defense, Personnel and Security Research Center, "Initiatives."
42. Zetter, "The Massive OPM Hack."
43. Hakamaa, "Adjudicating Background Investigations."
44. U.S. Department of Defense, Personnel and Security Research Center, "Initiatives."
45. U.S. Department of Defense Personnel and Security Research Center, "Initiatives."
46. Gillum and Tucker, "How Can Red Flags Be Missed?"
47. Gillum and Tucker, "How Can Red Flags Be Missed?" The article continues: "'The only thing that the security-clearance process is intended to protect is the security of the United States,' said Shlomo Katz, a government contracts lawyer who has been issued a clearance himself and is an expert on the process. 'The system is not designed to protect the lives of our co-workers, and therefore I don't view it as a failure of the system.'"
48. U.S. Department of Defense, Personnel and Security Research Center, "Initiatives."
49. The requirement for top-secret clearance was changed to five years under the tiered investigation policy adopted by the DNI but has not yet been fully implemented by the DoD at this writing in 2016.
50. *Federal Soup*, "Security Clearance Sabotage."
51. U.S. Department of Defense, Defense Security Service, "Industrial Personnel Security Clearance Process."
52. U.S. Department of Agriculture, Departmental Management, "PDSD homepage."
53. U.S. Department of Agriculture, Departmental Management, "PDSD homepage."
54. Executive Order 12968.
55. The full guidelines and mitigating factors are contained in the appendix.
56. Hopkins, "Underwater on the Mortgage."
57. Lunney, "Furloughs."
58. Jelinek, "Military Alcohol Abuse."
59. Lopez, "'Real Warriors' Takes Aim."
60. Silva-Braga, "When Navy SEAL Robert Guzzo Returned from Iraq." The specific concern about the clearance is in the *Washington Post* TV online interview, but not in the *Daily News* article by Knowles, cited below.
61. Knowles, "Navy SEAL's Parents."

62. Gillum and Tucker, "How Can Red Flags Be Missed?"
63. Sullivan, *Gatekeeper*, 89.
64. Lewis, "Navy Yard Gunman."
65. Drake sent the journalist email through Hushmail, an encrypted service. One of the ground rules he set at the beginning of their communication was that he would not reveal any sensitive or classified information (Mayer, "The Secret Sharer"). Gorman wrote several articles about waste, fraud, and abuse at the NSA and received an award from the Society of Professional Journalists for her series exposing government wrongdoing (Gorman, "NSA Officers Spy").
66. Gorman, "NSA Officers Spy."
67. "A Case that Could Be Overkill," *Washington Post*, editorial.
68. Kalson, "Muslim Physicist Leaves U.S."
69. O'Keefe, "Worker Suing Intelligence Agency."
70. Kalson, "Muslim Sues."
71. O'Keefe, "Worker Suing Intelligence Agency."
72. Esposito and Cole, "How Snowden Did It."
73. Wizner, "Defending Disclosure."

3. RUNNING AFOUL OF THE SYSTEM

1. U.S. Department of State, "All about Security Clearances."
2. Yang, "Vetting Company's Employees."
3. Braun, "U.S. Intelligence Officials."
4. Braun, "U.S. Intelligence Officials"; Suitability and Security Processes Review, "Problems with Face-to-Face Interviews."
5. Sullivan, *Gatekeeper*, 22. Sullivan points out that, in addition to Communism, the main focus of the polygraph program from its inception at the CIA was male homosexuality: "In the early years of CIA's polygraph program, polygraph tests focused on detecting Communists and homosexuals. Early tests had more questions dealing with Communism than other issues, but the homosexuality issue was pursued equally vigorously" (12).
6. Thompson, "It Has to Stop."
7. Shane, "Senate Blocks Change."
8. U.S. Department of Agriculture, Departmental Management, "PDSD homepage."
9. U.S. Congress, Office of Technology Assessment, "Scientific Validity of Polygraph."

10. U.S. Congress, Office of Technology Assessment, "Scientific Validity of Polygraph."
11. Executive Order 12968.
12. Starr, "The Interview."
13. Schmidt, Sanger, and Perlroth, "Chinese Hackers."
14. Philpott, "Military Update."
15. What is extraordinary about DIMHRS is not that the program was such a failure, but that the BTA was successful in killing it. Ten years of IT development failure and losses is not unusual in federal agencies as noted by David Powner, director of the GAO's information technology management issues, who testified before the House Committee on Oversight and Government Reform in 2013 "Federal IT projects 'too frequently incur cost overruns and schedule slippages while contributing little to mission-related outcomes. . . the federal government has achieved little of the productivity improvements that private industry has realized from IT'" (U.S. Government Accountability Officer, *Information Technology*).
16. For example, President-elect Obama promised new whistleblower protections during his administration on his transition website, stating, "Often the best source of information about waste, fraud, and abuse in government is an existing government employee committed to public integrity and willing to speak out. Such acts of courage and patriotism, which can sometimes save lives and often save taxpayer dollars, should be encouraged rather than stifled." But he took that site down after the transition was complete (Johnson, "Obama Promises").
17. Priest and Arkin, *Top Secret America*, 158.
18. The agencies referenced are the Defense Intelligence Agency (DIA), the Central Intelligence Agency (CIA), the National Reconnaissance Office (NRO), and the National Geospatial-Intelligence Agency (NGA).
19. Bowker and Starr, *Sorting Things Out*, 206.
20. Bowker and Starr, *Sorting Things Out*, 196.
21. Herzfeld, *The Social Production of Indifference*, 165.
22. Marisa Taylor at McClatchy Newspapers reported that Michael Pillsbury, a consultant, had to fight claims by CIA polygraphers that he admitted leaking sensitive information. Two things worked in his favor. He had the money for good lawyers, and he was not a federal employee. "With the help of some of Washington's top lawyers, Pillsbury realized he was a rare exception" (Taylor, "As Polygraph Screening Flourishes").

23. Gusterson, *Nuclear Rites*, 85.
24. Showtime, *Homeland*.
25. Kafka, *The Trial*, 114.
26. Bird and Sherwin, *American Prometheus*, 482.
27. Kafka, *The Trial*, 115.
28. Bird and Sherwin, *American Prometheus*, 483. In his account of the security clearance hearing, Richard Polenberg says there was an outward appearance of fairness for the uninitiated, but that it was Kafkaesque for those involved. "Yet if the 'odious courtesies,' as Kafka would have called them, were fully observed, the hearing in truth lacked fundamental elements of due process, the most egregious example being the surveillance of Oppenheimer by the FBI, which began on January 1, 1954" (Polenberg, *In the Matter of J. Robert Oppenheimer*, xviii).
29. Bizarro was a fictional supervillain who first appeared in DC Comics. In his world, up is down; down is up. He says "hello" when he leaves, "goodbye" when he arrives. The *Seinfeld* reference is to the episode "Bizarro Jerry," which refers extensively to Bizarro the comic book character.
30. Kafka, *In the Penal Colony*, 145.
31. Foucault, *Discipline and Punish*, 203.
32. Gusterson found that internalized surveillance had a chilling effect on laboratory employees signing petitions. In one example, a scientist who tried to circulate a petition protesting new drug-testing rules found many other scientists sympathetic but too nervous to sign because they feared their clearance might be revoked (*Nuclear Rites*, 86).
33. Priest and Arkin, *Top Secret America*, 159.
34. Gibson, "Spouses' Classified Access."
35. Gorman, "NSA Officers Spy."
36. Gallagher, "How NSA Spies."
37. Concerned Foreign Service Officers, "Concerned Foreign Service Officers Factsheet."
38. Weber, *The Protestant Ethic*.
39. Herzfeld, *The Social Production of Indifference*, 17.
40. Shils, *The Torment of Secrecy*, 15.

4. RECOMMENDATIONS FOR A BETTER SYSTEM

1. Bowker and Starr also remind us, "We walk here in a line similar to that of Hannah Arendt in her *Eichmann in Jerusalem: A Report on the Banality of Evil* (1963). The quiet bureaucrat 'just following orders'

is in a way more chilling than the expected monster dripping with grue." Eichmann explained what he was doing in routine, almost clerical terms; this was fully embedded in the systematic genocide of the Holocaust" (Bowker and Starr, *Sorting Things Out*, 196).

2. U.S. Merit Systems Protection Board, *Managing Public Employees*.
3. Frank, *Unfriendly Fire*.
4. Sieber, *Fatal Remedies*, 80, 81.
5. Rein, "The Agency That's Supposed to Protect Whistleblowers."
6. *U.S. vs. Scheffer* was the first case in which the Supreme Court issued a ruling on use of polygraph or "lie-detector," testing.
7. Katz, "Potential Blind Spots in Clearance Process."
8. Rein, "Want a Security Clearance?"
9. Sissela Bok warns against putting too much trust in technological approaches: "If implemented, [they] may offer yet another version of the Maginot Line; a set of fortifications erected at great human and commercial cost that gives a false sense of security" (Bok, *Secrets*, 152).
10. Philpott, "Military Update."
11. Office of the Director of National Intelligence, "2014 Report."
12. Report of the Commission on Protecting and Reducing Government Secrecy.
13. Committee on Oversight and Government Reform, U.S. House of Representatives, "Slipping Through the Cracks."
14. Office of Management and Budget, "Suitability and Security."
15. See, for example, the Intelligence Authorization Bill for Fiscal Year 2015 (S. 2741, sec. 311), which would require the director of national intelligence to prepare a report "describing proposals to improve the declassification process throughout the intelligence community." Another bill was introduced, HR 5240, that would require the president "to establish a goal for the reduction of classified information by not less than 10 percent within five years through improved declassification and improved original and derivative classification decision-making."
16. Johnson, "Obama Promises."
17. In 2014 the Department of Justice alleged that a major federal contractor, USIS, "flushed" or did not complete 665,000 background investigations that were required to grant clearances (Davenport, "Another Blow for USIS").
18. Max Weber argues that ascetic Protestantism was one of the major "elective affinities" in determining the rise of capitalism, bureaucracy, and the nation-state (*The Protestant Ethic*). Edward Shils points to

Puritanical origins of the personnel security screening process and its disdain for privacy as a phenomenon of religious revivalism where "privacy is waywardness . . . and waywardness is wickedness" (*The Torment of Secrecy*, 207). Shils, in his search for the roots of McCarthyism and its covalent hysteria in America, came to the conclusion that we are predisposed to such mean-spirited behaviors by a "nativist tradition" that has been with us since the founding of the country.

19. See Scott McClellan's book *What Happened*, which describes what government spokespeople sometimes endure.

20. Carroll, *House of War*, 306.

21. Fry, "Millennials Surpass Gen Xers."

22. Giddens, *Durkheim in Politics*, 38.

BIBLIOGRAPHY

Allen, Greg. "Mission Diversify: CIA Begins LGBT Recruiting." National Public Radio, December 2, 2012.

Apple, R. W. "25 Years Later; Lessons from the Pentagon Papers." *New York Times*, June 23, 1996.

Becker, Andrew. "Doubts about Polygraphs Don't Stop Federal Agencies from Using Them." Center for Investigative Reporting, April 4, 2013.

Bernstein, Walter. *Inside Out: A Memoir of the Blacklist*. Cambridge MA: Da Capo Press, 2007.

Bérubé, Allan. *Coming Out under Fire: The History of Gay Men and Women in World War Two*. New York: Free Press, 1990.

Bird, Kai, and Martin J. Sherwin. *American Prometheus: The Triumph and Tragedy of J. Robert Oppenheimer*. New York: Knopf, 2005.

Bok, Sissela. *Secrets: On the Ethics of Concealment and Revelation*. New York: Random House, 1983.

Bowker, Geoffrey, and Susan Starr. *Sorting Things Out: Classification and Its Consequences*. Cambridge MA: MIT Press, 2000.

Braun, Stephen. "U.S. Intelligence Officials to Monitor Federal Employees with Security Clearances." Associated Press, March 10, 2014.

Carroll, James. *House of War: The Pentagon and the Disastrous Rise of American Power*. Boston: Houghton Mifflin, 2006.

Clark, Charles S. "Pentagon's Key Whistle Blower Counselor Moves to Intel Community." *Government Executive*, July 29, 2013.

Code of Federal Regulations, Title 32—National Defense, Volume: 1, Date: 2013-07-01, Title: Subchapter F—Security, Context: Title 32—National Defense. Subtitle A—Department of Defense. Chapter I—Office

of the Secretary of Defense, Subchapter F—Security, Pt. 154, Part
154—Department of Defense Personnel Security Program Regulation.

Collins, Ronald K.L., "Benjamin Bache & The Fight for a Free Press. www
.firstamendment.org.

Committee on Oversight and Government Reform, U.S. House of Rep-
resentatives. "Slipping through the Cracks: How the D.C. Navy Yard
Shooting Exposes Flaws in the Federal Security Clearance Process."
Staff Report, Committee on Oversight and Government Reform, U.S.
House of Representatives, 113th Congress, February 11, 2013. https://
oversight.house.gov/wp-content/uploads/2014/02/Aaron-Alexis-Report
-FINAL.pdf.

Concerned Foreign Service Officers. "Concerned Foreign Services Officers
Factsheet." http://worldcrafters.com.

Currier, Cora. "Charting Obama's Crackdown on National Security Leaks."
ProPublica, July 30, 2013.

Davenport, Christian. "Another Blow for USIS as GAO Rules for Competi-
tor." *Washington Post*, October 21, 2014.

Deutscher, Irwin. *Accommodating Diversity: National Policies That Prevent
Ethnic Conflict.* New York: Lexington Books, 2002.

Editorial. "A Case that Could Be Overkill against a Whistleblower," *Washington
Post*, June 5, 2011. https://www.washingtonpost.com/opinions/a-case-that
-could-be-overkill-against-a-whistleblower/2011/06/03/AG2DemJH_story
.html.

Employee Polygraph Protection (EPP). 29 U.S. Code, chapter 22.

Employment of Homosexuals and Other Sex Perverts in Government (1950).
Interim Report submitted to the Committee on Expenditures in the
Executive Departments by Its Subcommittee on Investigations Pur-
suant to S. Res. 280 (81st Congress). A Resolution Authorizing the
Committee on Expenditures in the Executive Departments to Carry
Out Certain Duties.

Esposito, Richard, and Matthew Cole. "How Snowden Did It." CBS News,
August 26, 2013.

Executive Order 9835 of March 21, 1947. Prescribing Procedures for the
Administration of an Employees Loyalty Program in the Executive
Branch of the Government. http://trumanlibrary.org/executiveorders
/index.php?pid=502.

Executive Order 10450 of April 27, 1953. Security Requirements for Government Employment. 3 CFR (1949–1953). http://www.archives.gov
/federal-register/codification/executive-order/10450.html.

Executive Order 12968 of August 4, 1995. Revised Adjudicative Guidelines for Determining Eligibility for Access to Classified Information. 32 CFR, part 147 (1995). http://fas.org/sgp/clinton/eo12968.html.

Federal Soup (blog). "Directive Extends Whistleblower Protections to Intelligence Employees." October 11, 2012.

——. "Failed FBI Polygraph." January 2011. https://federalsoup.federal daily.com/forum_posts.asp?TID=31015&title=failed-fbi-polygraph.

——. "Security Clearance Sabotage." September 29, 2007. https://forum .federalsoup.com.

Forensic Toxicology Drug Testing Laboratory at Fort George G. Meade Maryland. "The History of Drug Testing in the Military." https://iftdtl .amedd.army.mil/ftmd/History.html.

Foucault, Michel. Discipline and Punish. New York: Pantheon Books, 1978.

Frank, Nathaniel. Unfriendly Fire: How the Gay Ban Undermines the Military and Weakens America. New York: Thomas Dunne, 2009.

Frieden, Terry. "Ex-State Official, Wife Accused of Spying for Cuba." CNN, June 9, 2009. http://www.cnn.com/2009/US/06/05/us.cuba.spies/.

Fry, Richard. "Millennials Surpass Gen Xers as the Largest Generation in U.S. Labor Force." Pew Research Center, May 11, 2015.

Gallagher, Ryan. "How NSA Spies Abused Their Powers to Snoop on Girlfriends, Lovers, and First Dates." Slate, September 27, 2013.

Gibson, Caitlin. "Spouses' Classified Access Keeps Abuse Victims Quiet." Washington Post, May 19, 2014.

Giddens, Anthony. Durkheim in Politics and the State. Stanford CA: Stanford University Press, 1986.

Gillum, Jack, and Eric Tucker. "How Can Red Flags Be Missed Like Navy Shooter's?" Associated Press, September 19, 2013.

Gladchuck, John Hollywood and Anticommunism: HUAC and the Evolution of the Red Menace, 1935–1950. New York: Routledge, 2009.

Gorman, Siobhan. "NSA Officers Spy on Love Interests." Wall Street Journal, August 23, 2013.

Grand, Gabriel. "Edward Snowden: A Private Contractor Gave Snowden His Security Clearance—and Missed the Red Flags." Policy.Mic, June 22, 2013. http://mic.com/articles/50417/edward-snowden-a-private-contrac tor-gave-snowden-his-security-clearance-and-missed-the-red-flags#. 05CwzzSyf.

Greenwald, Glenn. "On the Espionage Act Charges against Edward Snowden." The Guardian, June 22, 2013.

Gusterson, Hugh. *Nuclear Rites: A Weapons Laboratory at the End of the Cold War.* Berkeley: University of California Press, 1998.

Hakamaa, Marko. "Adjudicating Background Investigations—Not an Easy Job." ClearanceJobs.com, December 8, 2013.

Harnden, Toby. "The Spies Who Loved . . . and Lost Their Jobs." *Daily Telegraph,* June 7, 2007.

Herzfeld, Michael. *The Social Production of Indifference: Exploring the Symbolic Roots of Western Bureaucracy.* Chicago: University of Chicago Press, 1992.

Hopkins, Jamie Smith. "Underwater on the Mortgage, Stationed Away from Home, for Service Members Caught by the Housing Bust, Transfer Means a Home They Can't Easily Sell." *Baltimore Sun,* July 14, 2012.

Howard, Katie. "What Federal Applicants Should Know About Polygraph Tests." Federal News Radio, December 11, 2012.

Intelligence Authorization Bill for Fiscal Year 2015 (S. 2741, sec. 311).

Intelligence Reform and Terrorism Prevention Act of 2004, Pub. L. No. 108–458 (2004).

Jelinek, Pauline. "Military Alcohol Abuse 'Culture' Is Now a 'Crisis,' Report Finds." *Huffington Post,* September 17, 2012.

Johnson, David K. *The Lavender Scare: The Cold War Persecution of Gays and Lesbians in the Federal Government.* Chicago: University of Chicago Press, 2006.

Johnson, Luke. "Obama Promises, Including Whistleblower Protections, Disappear from Website." *Huffington Post,* July 26, 2013.

Joint Security and Suitability Reform Team. "Security and Suitability Process Reform." Initial Report, April 30, 2008. https://www.whitehouse.gov/sites/default/files/omb/assets/omb/reports/reform_plan_report_2008.pdf.

Kafka, Franz. *In the Penal Colony.* 17th ed. New York: Schocken Books, 1971.

———. *The Trial.* New Translation Based on the Restored text. New York: Schocken Books, 1998.

Kalson, Sally. "Muslim Physicist Leaves U.S. after Losing Security Clearance." *Pittsburgh Post-Gazette,* November 28, 2008.

———. "Muslim Sues over Loss of Security Clearance. *Pittsburgh Post-Gazette,* June 27, 2008.

Katz, Andrew. "Potential Blind Spots in Clearance Process That Gave Snowden Top-Secret Access." *Time,* June 15, 2013. http://nation.time.com/2013/06/15/potential-blind-spots-in-clearance-that-gave-snowden-top-secret-access/.

Knowles, David. "Navy SEAL's Parents Link Son's Suicide to Horrors of War, Stigma Surrounding Mental Health." *New York Daily News*, January 10, 2013.

LaFlure, Rebecca. "Security Clearance Lapses Stemmed from Washington's Heedless Emphasis on Speed over Quality Profits and Politics, Plus a Huge and Sudden Growth in Secrecy-Obsessed Institutions, Played Key Roles in Misguided Clearance Decisions." Center for Public Integrity, October 1, 2013. https://www.publicintegrity.org.

Lewis, Paul. "Navy Yard Gunman Given Security Clearance Despite 'Lie' about Arrest: Aaron Alexis, Who Shot Dead 12, Was Given Secret-Level Security Clearance despite Omission from Application Form." *The Guardian*, September 23, 2013.

Loftus, Joseph A. "Miller Convicted in Contempt Case." *New York Times*, June 2, 1957

Lopez, Todd. "'Real Warriors' Takes Aim at Mental Health Stigma." http://www.govexec.com/pay-benefits/2013/03/furloughs-could-endanger-feds-security-clearances/62101/. May 21, 2009.

Lunney, Kellie. "Furloughs Could Endanger Feds' Security Clearances." *Government Executive*, March 26, 2013.

Marcus, Ruth. "The Insufferable Snowden." *Washington Post*, January 1, 2014.

Mayer, Jane. "The Secret Sharer: Is Thomas Drake an Enemy of the State?" *New Yorker*, May 23, 2011.

McClellan, Scott. *What Happened*. New York: Perseus, 2008.

McHugh, John M. *Army Directive 2013-18 (Army Insider Threat Program)*, July 31, 2012.

Miller, Arthur. *The Crucible*. New York: Viking Press, 1953.

National Center for Credibility Assessment. "PDD Program." http://www.ncca.mil/pdd_program_about.htm.

National Research Council of the National Academies of Science, Engineering and Medicine. *The Polygraph and Lie Detection*. Committee to Review the Scientific Evidence on the Polygraph, Board on Behavioral, Cognitive, and Sensory Sciences and Committee on National Statistics, Division of Behavioral and Social Sciences and Education. Washington DC: National Academies Press, 2014.

Navy Drug Screening Laboratory, San Diego. "Frequently Asked Questions." http://www.med.navy.mil/sites/sandiegodruglab/Pages/faq.aspx.

Office of the Director of National Intelligence. "2014 Report on Security Clearance Determinations," January 2015. http://www.dni.gov/files

/documents/2015-4-21%20Annual%20Report%20on%20Security%20
Clearance%20Determinations.pdf.

Office of Management and Budget. "Suitability and Security Processes
Review." Report to the President, February 2014. http://www.fas.org
/sgp/othergov/omb/suitsec-2014.pdf.

O'Keefe, Ed. "Worker Suing Intelligence Agency Claims Anti-Muslim
Bias." *Washington Post*, November 1, 2011.

Panetta, Leon. Speech to Defense Department Employees, June 15, 2012.

Philpott, Tom. "Military Update: Mullen Pulls Plug on Problem-Plagued
DIMHRS Pay Program." *Hampton Roads Daily Press*, February 21, 2010.

Polenberg, Richard. *In the Matter of J. Robert Oppenheimer: The Security
Clearance Hearing*, Ithaca NY: Cornell University Press, 2002.

Polygraph Investigative Services. "FAQs." http://www.polygraphis.com
/WebsiteFAQ.htm.

Popkin, Jim. "Ana Montes Did Much Harm Spying for Cuba. Chances Are,
You Haven't Heard of Her." *Washington Post Magazine*, April 18, 2013.

Poulsen, Kevin, and Kim Zetter. "U.S. Intelligence Analyst Arrested in
WikiLeaks Video Probe." *Wired*, June 6, 2010.

Priest, Dana, and William Arkin. *Top Secret America: The Rise of the New
American State*. New York: Little, Brown, 2011.

Pressly, Linda. "The Spy Who Loved Her." *The Guardian*, November 18,
2004.

Rapid Clear. "Detox Pills." http://www.rapidcleardetox.com/detox-pills
.aspx.

Rein, Lisa. "The Agency That's Supposed to Protect Whistleblowers across
the Government Got Slapped for Retaliating against One of Its
Own." *Washington Post*, October 2, 2014.

———. "Want a Security Clearance? Feds Will Now Check Your Facebook
and Twitter First." *Washington Post*, May 13, 2016.

Report of the Commission on Protecting and Reducing Government
Secrecy (the Moynihan Secrecy Commission). Created under Title
IX of the Foreign Relations Authorization Act for Fiscal Years 1994
and 1995 (P.L. 103-236 SEC. 900), 1994. http://www.fas.org/sgp/library
/moynihan/foreword.html.

Rhem, Kathleen T. "Who's Doing What, and How They Get Caught: A
Look at Drug Use and Testing within the Military." *American Forces
Press Service*, Washington, November 26, 2001.

Sartre, Jean-Paul. "Mad Beasts." In *Selected Prose: The Writings of Jean-
Paul Sartre,* pp. 207–11. Evanston IL: Northwestern University Press,

1974. Originally published as "Les Animaux malades de la rage" in *Libération*, June 22, 1953.

Schmidt, Michael, S. David E. Sanger, and Nicole Perlroth. "Chinese Hackers Pursue Key Data on U.S. Workers." *New York Times*, July 9, 2014.

Schmitt, Eric. "C.I.A. Warning on Snowden in '09 Said to Slip through the Cracks." *New York Times*, October 10, 2013.

Shafer, Jack. "Who Said It First? Journalism Is the 'First Rough Draft of History.'" *Slate*, August 30, 2010.

Shane, Leo, II. "Senate Blocks Change to Military Sex Assault Cases." *Marine Corps Times*, March 6, 2014.

Shils, Edward A. *The Torment of Secrecy: The Background and Consequences of American Security Policies*. Chicago: Ivan R. Dee, 1956.

Showtime. *Homeland*. http://www.sho.com/sho/search?q=homeland.

Sieber, Sam. *Fatal Remedies: The Ironies of Social Intervention*. 1st ed. Boston: Springer, 1981.

Silva-Braga, Brook. "When Navy SEAL Robert Guzzo Returned from Iraq, He Feared Seeking Treatment for PTSD Would Endanger His Career." *The Fold / Washington Post*, January 9, 2013.

Simpson, Alan K., and Rodger E. McDaniel. "Prologue." In *Dying for Joe McCarthy's Sins: The Suicide of Wyoming Senator Lester Hunt*. Cody WY: Wordsworth Press, 2013.

Sledge, Matt. "Unhappy with U.S. Foreign Policy? Pentagon Says You Might Be a 'High Threat.'" *Huffington Post*, August 7, 2013.

Starr, Douglas. "The Interview: Do Police Interrogation Techniques Produce False Confessions?" *New Yorker*, December 9, 2013.

Stein, Jeff. "Lie Detectors Lie (Tell the C.I.A.). *New York Times*, February 19, 1995.

Suitability and Security Processes Review. "Problems with Face-to-Face Interviews." A Report to the President, February 2014. https://www.whitehouse.gov/sites/default/files/omb/reports/suitability-and-security-process-review-report.pdf.

Sullivan, John. *Gatekeeper: Memoirs of a CIA Polygraph Examiner*. Washington DC: Potomac Books, 2007.

Taylor, Marisa. "As Polygraph Screening Flourishes, Critics Say Oversight Abandoned." McClatchy Newspapers, December 6, 2012.

———. "FBI Turns Away Many Applicants Who Fail Lie-Detector Tests." McClatchy Newspapers, May 20, 2013.

———. "Sen. Charles Grassley Seeks Probe of Polygraph Techniques at National Reconnaissance Office." McClatchy Newspapers, July 27, 2012.

Taylor, Marisa, and Jonathan S. Landay. "Obama's Crackdown Views Leaks as Aiding Enemies of U.S." McClatchy News Service, June 20, 2013.

Thompson, Mark. "It Has to Stop: A Rape Case Reveals an Unbalanced Military-Justice System." *Time*, September 16, 2013.

Tully, Mathew B. "Know the Right Thing to Do When Your Drug Test Is Wrong." *Army Times*, August 27, 2007.

U.S. Congress, Office of Technology Assessment. "Scientific Validity of Polygraph Testing: A Research Review and Evaluation." A Technical Memorandum, Washington DC (OTA-TM-H-15), November 1983. http://www.fas.org/sgp/othergov/polygraph/ota/.

U.S. Department of Agriculture, Departmental Management. "PDSD homepage." http://www.dm.usda.gov/ocpm/SecurityGuideEmployees/SelfReporting.htm.

U.S. Department of Defense, Counterintelligence Field Activity. *Federal Psychophysiol Detection of Deception Examiner Handbook*, October 2, 2006. https://antipolygraph.org/documents/federal-polygraph-handbook-02-10-2006.pdf.

U.S. Department of Defense, Defense Security Service. "Electronic Fingerprint Capture Options for Industry," Version 4.0. February 2014.

———. "Industrial Personnel Security Clearance Process, Processing an Applicant for an Industrial Personnel Security Clearance." http://www.dss.mil/psmo-i/indus_psmo-i_process_applicant.html.

———. "Joint Personnel Adjudication System (JPAS)." http://www.dss.mil/diss/jpas/jpas.html.

U.S. Department of Defense, Office of Inspector General. "Frequently Asked Questions: Drug Screening." http://www.dodig.mil/Careers/faq.html#Q1.2.

U.S. Department of Defense, Personnel and Security Research Center. "Initiatives." http://www.dhra.mil/perserec/currentinitiatives.html.

———. "Hanssen: Deep Inner Conflicts." Defense Human Resources Activity; Office of the Inspector General, *A Review of the FBI's Performance in Deterring, Detecting, and Investigating the Espionage Activities of Robert Philip Hanssen*. Washington DC: Department of Justice, 2003.

U.S. Department of Justice. *A Review of FBI Security Programs Commission for Review of FBI Security Programs*. Washington DC, March 2002.

U.S. Department of Labor, Office of the Assistant Secretary for Policy. "elaws—Employment Laws Assistance for Workers and Small Businesses: Drug-Free Workplace Advisor." http://www.dol.gov/elaws/drugfree.htm.

U.S. Department of State. "All about Security Clearances." http://www
.state.gov/m/ds/clearances/c10978.htm.

U.S. Government Accountability Office. *Information Technology: OMB and Agencies Need to More Effectively Implement Major Initiatives to Save Billions of Dollars: Statement of David A. Powner, Director, Information Technology Management Issues* (GAO-13-796T) http://www.gao
.gov/assets/660/656191.pdf.

U.S. Merit Systems Protection Board. *Managing Public Employees in the Public Interest.* Report to the President and the Congress of the United States, January 2013. http://www.mspb.gov/appeals/whistleblower.htm.

U.S. vs. Scheffer, 1998. 523 U.S. 303.

Weber, Max. *The Protestant Ethic and the Spirit of Capitalism.* New York: Routledge, 1930.

Weiner, Tim. "Why I Spied: Aldrich Ames." *New York Times,* July 31, 1994.

Wise, Lindsay. "Contractor Responsible for Snowden's Security Clearance Investigated for Inadequate Background Checks." McClatchy Washington Bureau, June 20, 2013.

Wizner, Ken. "Defending Disclosure." *Stand* 1, no. 2 (Summer 2014). American Civil Liberties Union Foundation, New York.

Yang, Jia Lynn. "Vetting Company's Employees Felt Stress." *Washington Post,* September 21, 2013.

Yenne, Bill. *Rising Sons: The Japanese American GIs Who Fought for the United States in World War II.* New York: St. Martin's Press, 2007.

Zetter, Kim. "The Massive OPM Hack Actually Hit 21 Million People." *Wired,* July 9, 2015.

———. "Security Jolt in Wikileaks Case: Feds Found Manning-Assange Chat Logs on Laptop." *Wired,* December 19, 2011.

INDEX

access to classified information.
See classified information,
determination of eligibility for
access to
ACES (Automated Continuing
Evaluation System), 36
Adams, John, 2
Adjudication Decision Support
(ADS) System, 37–38
Adjudicative Guidelines for
Determining Eligibility for
Access to Classified
Information: Code of Federal
Regulations, 129–31; overview
of, 43–44; Subpart A—
Adjudication, 131–44; Subpart
B—Investigative Standards,
144–51; Subpart C—Guidelines
for Temporary Access,
152–53
adjudicators, role of, 37, 39, 42
administrative leave, 91, 96
ADS (Adjudication Decision
Support) System, 37–38
agreement on need for clearance,
xiv, 58–60

alcohol consumption, 45, 88,
139–40
Alexis, Aaron, 16, 39, 50, 51
Alien Act of 1797, 2
allegiance to U.S., 44, 133–34
Ames, Aldrich, 12–13, 32
anxiety, feelings of, 86, 90, 95–96
apartheid system of classification,
89
appeals of revocation of
clearances, 93–94, 119–20
Arkin, William, 83
Army: Insider Threat Program,
19; polygraph exams and, 28
Atomic Energy Commission, 4
Automated Continuing
Evaluation System (ACES), 36

Bache, Benjamin Franklin, 2
background investigations: limits
on, 65–67; overview of, 23–25;
problems with, 62–65
Barber, Michael, 8
beating polygraph exams, 34
Becker, Andrew, 29
benefits of security clearances, 83

loss of security clearances. *See* revocation of clearances
love, spying for, 11–12
Loyalty Order, 5–6
LX4000 polygraph instruments, 33–34
Lykken, David, 34

Manhattan Project, 3, 4
Manning, Chelsea Elizabeth, 16–17, 19, 34
Marines, support establishment of, 82
Marks, Anne Wilson, 98
Marks, Herbert S., 98
marriage and security clearances, 54, 65–66, 90–91, 105
mass-surveillance programs, 14–15
McCarthy, Joseph Raymond, 5
McClatchy Newspapers, 29, 30, 31, 34
McHugh, John M., 19
mental illness, 16, 49–51, 141–42. *See also* personality disorders
Merit Systems Protection Board, 10, 114, 116
methodology, xiii–xiv
military members: alcohol and drug addiction of, 49; change of duty stations and, 47–48; homosexual, 7, 115; psychological conditions and, 49–51
millennials in labor force, 127
Miller, Arthur, xiv
money, spying for, 12–13
Montes, Ana Belén, 15

moral reasons for spying, 15
Moynihan, Patrick, 123
Myers, Walter Kendall and Gwendolyn, 15

National Academy of Sciences, on polygraph exams, 32, 69, 120
National Center for Credibility Assessment (NCCA): polygraph exams and, 28; Psychophysiological Detection of Deception Program, 30, 31–32, 34
National Industrial Security Program, xii
"National Insider Threat Policy and Minimum Standards for Executive Branch Insider Threat Programs," 18–19
nationalism, 104
national origin, as security threat, 9–10
National Reconnaissance Office, 31
national security, threats to: ethnicity and national origin, 9–10; evolution of, 20; insider threats, 18–19, 36, 42, 102–3; as multifaceted, 1–2
National Security Agency (NSA): IT security methods of, 54–55; misuse of classified information by officers of, 106; surveillance programs of, 14–15
National Security Decision Directive 84, 71

Navy: Drug Screening Laboratory, 26; policies for homosexual personnel of, 7

Navy Yard shootings, 16, 38, 51, 123–24

NCCA. *See* National Center for Credibility Assessment

neighbors, as references, 24, 64, 121

Nixon administration and Pentagon Papers, 14

normative perception surrounding clearances, 84–85

NSA. *See* National Security Agency

number of secrets and clearances, reducing, 123–24

oaths of allegiance of federal workers, 14–15

Obama, Barack: Espionage Act and, 19–20; insider threats and, 18–19, 36, 42, 102; on nondiscrimination in military, 8; Presidential Policy Directive 19, 17; Snowden and, 14; whistleblowers and, 124–25

Office of Personnel Management (OPM): hack of ACES system and, 36; hack of e-QIP and, 80, 122

Office of Technology Assessment, 69, 120

Office of the Director of National Intelligence, 121

online profiles. *See* social media

Oppenheimer, J. Robert, 3–4, 98–99

Outserve, 8

outside activities, 46, 52–54, 143

Panetta, Leon, 8

Panopticon, 100

Pearl Harbor, attack on, 9

peer surveillance, 42, 102–3

Pentagon Papers, 13–14

periodic reinvestigations, 41

personal conduct, 45, 137–138

personality disorders: assessment tool for, 16, 122; guidelines on, 141–42; security clearances for persons with, 38–39

Personnel and Research Center (PERSEREC), 35, 36, 37–38, 40

personnel security clearance system: agreement on need for, xiv, 58–60; assumptions of, 1; benefits of, 83; capitalism and, xiv; databases for, 35–40; defects of, xiv–xv; experiences with, xiii, 57–58; impact of, xi, xii; of Oppenheimer, 3–4; overview of, xi, 125–26; prediction of human behavior and, 10–11; process of going through, 21–23; streamlining, 35; urinalyses, 25–27. *See also* background investigations; flaws in system; impact of experiences with clearance system; incident reports; polygraph exams; recommendations for improvement

phobic reactions to polygraph exams, 77

stress: anxiety and, 86, 90, 95–96; of being held in limbo, 90–91, 92; of dealing with system, 61, 68–69; depression and, 83–84, 86, 90–91, 95–96; polygraph exams and, 73–75; power and weight of bureaucratic wrath and, 126–27

Sullivan, John, 50–51, 65

suspension of security clearances, 41. *See also* revocation of clearances

SWFT (Secure Web Fingerprint Transmission), 35, 36

Taylor, Melisa, 33–34

technology. *See* information technology (IT) systems; polygraph exams

temporary access, guidelines for, 152–53

Textron, 82

Thomas, Clarence, 120

time limit for appeal process, 120

traits of spies, 13

The Trial (Kafka), 97, 98

true believers, 15

Truman, Harry S, Executive Order 9835, 5–6

Tucker, Eric, 38–40, 50

Tully, Matthew, 26

type I and type II errors, 58, 69

urinalyses, 25–27

U.S. Agency for International Development, xii

U.S. Investigations Services, 25, 62

Voice of America, xii

war relocation camps, 9, 115

Weber, Max, xiv, 109, 110

whistleblowers: financial hardships and, 93–94; "good-bad" binary and, 111; handling protected information and, 51–52; leadership and, 81–82; loss of professional identity and community of, 84–85; Obama administration and, 17–18, 124–25; reinstatement of clearances and, 99; retaliation by government on, 115–17, 118

"whole person approach," 71, 72, 91

WikiLeaks, 17, 19

Wilson, Woodrow, 2–3

Woolsey, R. James, 13

World War I, 3

World War II, 3, 9

www.ingramcontent.com/pod-product-compliance
Lightning Source LLC
Chambersburg PA
CBHW031259310326
41914CB00116B/1681/J